The Mycenaeans

The Mycenaeans

Louise Schofield

THE BRITISH MUSEUM PRESS

For Norman and Muriel Schofield

Louise Schofield has asserted the right to be identified
as the author of this work

First published in 2007 by The British Museum Press
A division of The British Museum Company Ltd
38 Russell Square, London WC1B 3QQ
www.britishmuseum.co.uk

ISBN-13   978-0-7141-2090-4
ISBN-10   0-7141-20904

A catalogue record for this book is available from the
British Library

Title page: Women riding in a chariot to watch the hunt
on a fresco from Tiryns (see fig. 79).

Contents

Introduction

Heinrich Schliemann's extraordinary excavations on the acropolis of Mycenae in 1876 began the discovery of a great lost civilization, that of the Greeks of the Late Bronze Age (c.1600–1100 BC), a people we call the Mycenaeans. Having found the city of Troy, and fabulous treasure within its walls, Schliemann had turned his attentions to Mycenae in his quest for the burial site of the great king Agamemnon himself, leader of the Greek expedition against Troy. The circle of graves he found just inside the monumental Lion Gate had kept the secret of their contents safe for almost three and a half thousand years. Digging deep down into the earth Schliemann revealed the burials of men wearing heavy gold face masks and gold funerary armour, and equipped with an impressive array of weapons; women in massive gold crowns and bedecked with jewellery; and babies wrapped head to toe in sheet gold foil. These were the élite of a warrior people with a sophisticated and complex society, whose story takes us not only to Greece, but to Egypt, the East, to many lands of the Mediterranean and perhaps even, eventually, to the walls of Troy itself.

The land in which the Mycenaeans lived did much to shape their history. It was one of rugged mountain ranges, wooded valleys and fertile plains, its coastline of bays and beaches giving easy access to the sea. Against this landscape the Mycenaeans flourished: they farmed the fertile soil, exploited the natural resources of their countryside and grew in wealth and power.

The food resources available to the Mycenaeans were rich in this Mediterranean climate: on the plains and lower hillsides they could grow cereals like barley, oats and wheat and pulses such as lentils, various kinds of beans and chickpeas. Olive and fig trees are native to Greece and would have been important sources of food, as were vines, which were already cultivated at this time. The villagers kept domesticated animals for food, such as pigs, goats, sheep and cattle, and hunted wild boar, deer and hare. The sea, rivers and streams would have provided a plentiful supply of fish. Analyses of the interiors of Mycenaean cooking pots have shown that the people ate a lot of meat, from both domesticated and wild animals, often cooked in olive oil with lentils and chickpeas.

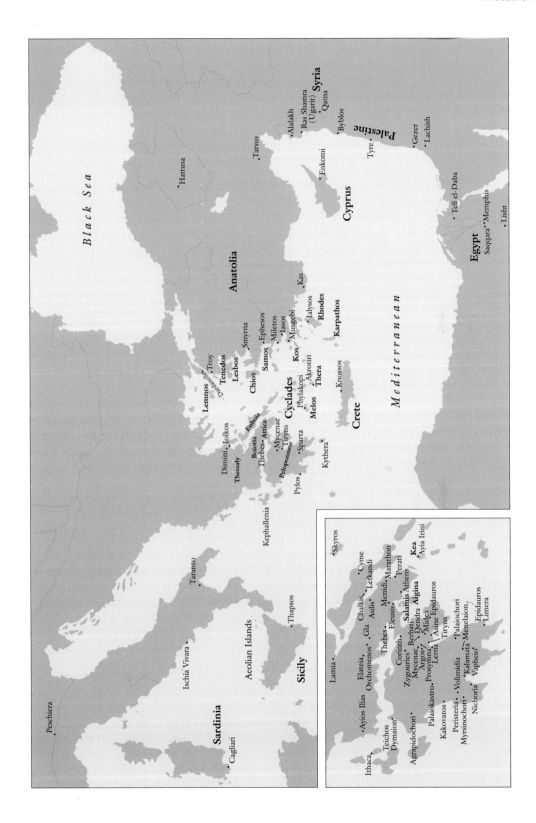

Black Sea

Syria

Ras Shamra
(Ugarit)
Qatna
Alalakh
Byblos
Palestine
Gezer
Lachish
Tyre
Enkomi
Cyprus
Tell el-Daba
Memphis
Egypt
Saqqara
Lisht

Hattusa

Tarsus

Anatolia

Kas

Smyrna
Ephesos
Miletos
Iasos
Musgebi
Ialysos
Rhodes
Karpathos

Troy
Tenedos
Lesbos
Chios
Samos
Kos
Akrotiri
Thera
Knossos

Lemnos
Dardanelles
Cyclades
Phylakopi
Melos

Crete

Mediterranean

Euboia
Iolkos
Dimini
Thessaly
Boiotia
Thebes Attica
Mycenae
Tiryns
Peloponnese Sparta
Pylos
Kythera

Kephallenia

Taranto

Thapsos

Ischia Vivara

Aeolian Islands

Sicily

Peschiera

Sardinia

Cagliari

Skyros

Cyme
Chalkis Lefkandi
Gla Aulis Menidi Marathon
Kea
Ayia Irini
Perati
Thebes Eleusis Salamis Athens
Corinth Berbati Aigina
Zygouries Dendra
Mycenae Midea
Argos Asine Epidauros
Prosymna Lerna Epidauros
Tiryns
Palaiochori
Peristeria Volimidia Menelaion Epidauros
Palaiokastro Limera
Agrapidochori Kalamata
Kakovatos Myrsinochori Vapheio
Teichos Nichoria
Ithaca Dymaion

Lamia
Ayios Ilias
Elateia
Orchomenos
Palaiokastro

7

The physical characteristics of their land helped to determine the extent of the great kingdoms that grew up within it, with tall mountain ranges and fast-flowing rivers making natural boundaries between them. The many safe natural harbours on the coast, together with the Mycenaeans' position between the lands of the east and west Mediterranean, facilitated contacts between the Mycenaeans and their neighbours, originally within the Aegean itself and later further afield. The trading links forged with these other countries were determined in part by the natural mineral resources available to the Mycenaeans at home (copper, for instance, and silver) and those that they lacked (notably tin with which to make bronze).

This book charts the story of the Mycenaeans, from their origins to their eventual fall. In its pages we will see how their discovery came about when Schliemann went in search of the truth behind Homer's two great epic poems, the *Iliad* and the *Odyssey*. We will follow him as he discovers the lost city of Troy and then goes to Mycenae to look for the tomb of the legendary king Agamemnon, where he finds a circle of graves containing men, women and children buried between 1600 and1450 BC. We will look at how the Mycenaeans lived in these early years, known as the Shaft Grave Era, before seeing them adopt a palace system from the Minoans on Crete and establish independent kingdoms across their land, ruled from finely built palaces, many of them protected by vast fortifications. From where they lived, where they buried their dead and how they worshipped their gods we will try to build up a picture of what kind of people the Mycenaeans were, and what kind of relationships they had with the peoples who lived in the lands around them. A series of catastrophes hit the Mycenaeans *c.*1200 BC, and although the culture continued for another century or so, Greece slipped finally into a Dark Age which lasted several hundred years. Out of this Dark Age, in the eighth century BC, Greece emerged with a network of myths and legends, telling tales of great kings, heroes, and battles, the greatest of all being the story of the Trojan War. In the final chapter of the book we will come back to the myths and legends that led to the original discovery of the Mycenaeans and ask the question: Did the Trojan War ever really take place?

New discoveries made in the past few decades, new scientific methods of asking questions from the past and a growing understanding of Mycenaean Greek have all helped in creating a fuller picture of these people than has hitherto been possible.

This book is not aimed at the specialist reader, but rather at the interested layman. Nor is it intended as a comprehensive study of the Mycenaeans and their material remains, though endnotes and recommended further reading will direct the reader to works that discuss certain elements in detail and cover the finer points of the many controversies that still surround the Mycenaeans and the Bronze Age world that they inhabited. Rather it aims to steer a course through these material remains and through the many controversies in an attempt to answer the question: Who were the Mycenaeans?

Author's note
In this book the Greek spellings have usually been used, except when referring to people and places of legend where the Latinized forms are more easily recognizable and familiar.

1

The Discovery of the Mycenaeans

The myths and legends of Classical Greece look back to a Golden Age of heroes, during which powerful kings ruled great palaces and mighty warriors fought fierce battles. Such tales, particularly that of the Trojan War, contained clues as to the existence of the long-lost Mycenaeans – clues which would eventually inspire one man to try and show the world that this was not legend at all, but history.

The story of Troy was told as part of a whole series of poems known as the Epic Cycle, the most famous of which were the *Iliad* and the *Odyssey*, attributed to the blind poet Homer and probably first written down in the late eighth century BC. The seeds of conflict, which were to lead eventually to ten long years of war, were sewn at the wedding of Peleus (king of Thessaly) and the nymph Thetis, when a golden apple inscribed with the words 'for the most beautiful' was thrown amongst the assembled goddesses. In the resulting beauty competition, three goddesses – Hera, Athena and Aphrodite – laid claim to the apple. Zeus sent the three goddesses to Troy to ask the shepherd prince Paris, son of the city's mighty king Priam, to decide. Hera told him he would have wealth and power if he chose her, Athena offered him prowess in battle and wisdom, and Aphrodite promised him the most beautiful woman in the world. Paris awarded the apple to Aphrodite, but the loveliest of all women was Helen, who was already married to Menelaus, king of Sparta. Undeterred, Paris visited Sparta, seduced Helen and took her back home with him to Troy.

The enraged Menelaus travelled to Mycenae and sought the help of his brother Agamemnon, king of that great city and overlord of all the Greeks. Agamemnon massed together warriors and their rulers from all the Greek lands and with a mighty fleet of a thousand ships they gathered at Aulis on the coast of Boiotia and set sail for Troy. Once there, they set up camp and besieged the city for ten years, before eventually tricking the Trojans with the gift of a large wooden horse. They left the horse, which had Greek warriors hidden inside it, on the Trojan Plain and pretended to sail away defeated. The Trojans took the horse within the walls of the city and when night fell the Greeks emerged and opened the gates of Troy to their compatriots, who had returned in the darkness. Thus Troy fell.

1. Roman marble portrait bust of the blind poet Homer, based on a Hellenistic original of around 200 BC.

WRITERS, TRAVELLERS AND ARTISTS

For the Classical Greeks and the Romans after them, the Trojan War was part of their history. The fifth-century BC Greek historian Thucydides, in the introduction to his work *The Peloponnesian War*, writes what he knows of the history of Greece before his own time. He accepts Agamemnon, overlord of the Achaean (Greek) expedition to Troy, as a historical figure: 'Agamemnon, it seems to me, must have been the most powerful of the rulers of his day.' He is not, however, impressed by the city of Mycenae itself, which was relatively small and of little importance at the time he was writing: 'Mycenae certainly was a small place, and many of the towns of that period do not seem to us today to be particularly imposing.'[1]

Other Classical Greek writers, though, were not as dismissive and were impressed by the great walls of Mycenae. They called them 'Cyclopean' after the Cyclopes, the one-eyed giants of the *Odyssey*, believing no mere mortals could have built them. Euripides, in his tragedies of the fifth century BC, makes frequent reference to the walls of Mycenae. In his play *Heracles* the eponymous hero cries out in a frenzy: 'I'm setting out against Mycenae. Bring crowbars and pickaxes; we'll lever up their strong Cyclopean masonry fitted with line and hammer – iron will prize it open.'[2]

This regard for the great cities of legend, and the belief that these legends were in fact history, persisted in Roman times. In the second century AD Pausanias, a Greek from Asia Minor, travelled around Greece recording the ancient remains he found and the tales associated with them. Of Mycenae he says: 'Still there are parts of the ring wall left, including the Gate with Lions standing on it. They say this is the work of Cyclopes, who built the wall of Tiryns for Proitos.' The nearby citadel of Tiryns exerted a similar fascination: 'If you go further and then turn off to the right you come to the ruins of Tiryns. Nothing is left of the ruins except the wall, which was built by Cyclopes with natural rocks, all so huge that a pair of mules would not even begin to shift the smallest.'[3]

From the fifteenth century onwards a few intrepid travellers from the lands of northern Europe reached Greece, intent on exploring its Classical remains. By the late eighteenth century they were arriving in greater numbers, drawn to the walls of roughly hewn stone they came across in the landscape and in particular to the monumental Lion Gate of Mycenae. Many wrote accounts of the sites as they found them, more deeply buried perhaps but otherwise little changed since Pausanias' day. One such visitor was François René de Chateaubriand, author of the *Itineraire de Paris à Jérusalem* (1811):

Crossing a barren valley, I saw the ruins of Mycenae on the side of a facing hill. I particularly admired one of the gates of the city fashioned out of gigantic blocks of stone that are set on the rock of the mountain itself and seem to form part of it. Two colossal lions carved on each side of the gate are its only ornament; these are represented in relief and stand on their hind legs looking outwards like the lions which support the coats of arms of our knights of old. The heads of the lions are missing. Not even in Egypt have I seen such imposing architecture and the desert which surrounds it adds still further to its grandeur.

Equally impressed was Englishman Christopher Wordsworth:

The ruins of Mycenae ... are in some respects unequalled in interest by any object in Greece. The walls of the citadel may be traced

2. Watercolour painting
of Mycenae by
Edward Dodwell.

in their entire circuit, and on the western side they rise to a considerable height. The interior of their enclosure, or area of the
citadel, is covered with the common turf and mountain plants of
the country.

Skilled artists were amongst those who journeyed through Greece and
their drawings and paintings have left an evocative record. An Englishman, Edward Dodwell, who first visited Greece in 1801, was particularly interested in ruins which he considered 'early'. He produced
a volume of some of his drawings entitled *Cyclopian, or Pelasgic Remains
in Greece and Italy* (1834), many of which have subsequently been identified as of Mycenaean sites. He reached Mycenae in 1806 and voices
his emotions on being there: 'I approached the Cyclopian city of Pelops
with a greater degree of veneration than any other place in Greece had
inspired.' His fine paintings and drawings of the most picturesque of
the ruins he found at Mycenae (the fortification walls, Lion Gate,
postern gate, Treasury of Atreus and Tomb of Clytemnestra) have left
a vivid pictorial record of the site in the early years of the nineteenth
century, as have his drawings of the nearby fortress of Tiryns and the
great tholos tomb at Orchomenos.

Most visitors to Mycenae were content to admire and to draw, but
a few portable elements of these monumental ruins nevertheless fell

prey to the collector's instinct. In 1802 Lord Elgin visited Mycenae and took home with him some fragments of the carved-stone decorative façade of the Treasury of Atreus. Other fragments from the same tomb façade were taken by the Marquis of Sligo in 1810, and both sets of fragments are now on display in the British Museum. Other Mycenaean objects also began to find their way into European collections, though they were not yet recognized for what they were. Mycenaean seals (engraved semi-precious stones), for instance, were displayed in museums together with Archaic and Classical Greek gems. In 1841 the Greek Archaeological Service partially cleared the Lion Gate, and in the 1860s and 1870s excavations were undertaken on the island of Rhodes which uncovered tombs containing vases, weapons and jewellery of a then unrecognized type, but now known to be Mycenaean.

The Mycenaeans had been lost and forgotten beneath the 'common turf and mountain plants' of Greece for almost three thousand years, but their secrets were about to be revealed. A German businessman, Heinrich Schliemann, was intent on proving the truth of his own conviction, namely that Homer's fabled city of Troy and the heroes who besieged it were more than simply poetic fiction.

3. The 'Treasury of Minyas' at Orchomenos before excavation, by Edward Dodwell, 1805.

4. Hissarlik (Troy) from the north-west, drawn in 1879.

SCHLIEMANN'S DISCOVERIES

Born in 1822 in Neubukow, Schliemann grew up in Mecklenburg, the son of a poor pastor. He became an extremely wealthy businessman, amassed a great fortune and then gave up the life of commerce to put his considerable energies and resources into archaeology.[4]

Following an initial visit to Greece, he went in search of the lost city of Troy, the legendary king Priam's palace citadel. Topographical studies comparing the position of Troy as described in the poems with the relevant area of the coast of modern Turkey, close to the entrance to the Dardanelles, had focused scholarly attention on a site called Bunarbashi. Schliemann dug a few trial trenches there with disappointing results and then, on the recommendation of an Englishman, Frank Calvert, turned his attentions to Hissarlik, some way further north, a part of which Calvert owned.

Hissarlik was a great mound dominating the surrounding plain, a tell site made up of city built upon ruined city over thousands of years. Schliemann dug exploratory trenches there in April 1870 and began full excavations at the site in October 1871. He dug great trenches right through the multiple layers in his hurry to find Priam's Troy, looking for the ruins of a city that would fit the description given in the Homeric poems. In 1873 he uncovered a sacked and burnt city with a stone fortification wall and a stone ramp leading up to a gateway, its remains buried under almost 3 m (10 ft) of fire-blackened debris. Identifying this as Priam's Troy he named the large house within the walls Priam's Palace and a fabulous treasure he discovered in the city – which

5. Sophia Schliemann wearing the 'Jewels of Helen', part of the treasure found by her husband in the ruins of Troy II.

included gold and silver vessels, jewellery of spectacular beauty and complexity and ceremonial hammer-axes of highly polished jade and lapis lazuli – Priam's Treasure. Although publicly claiming to have found Priam's Troy, Schliemann had his own doubts. He was disappointed with the small size and lack of splendour of his city and he could not equate the crudity of the pottery he found there with the civilized life led by Homer's Trojans. Subsequent excavations were to prove his doubts justified. Although he had indeed found Troy, he had dug too deep, reaching the level of the site now known as Troy II, dating to around 2600–2400 BC, some one thousand years or more too early to be associated with the legend of the Trojan War.[5]

Having displeased the Turkish authorities by his removal of the Trojan treasure to Athens, Schliemann left Troy and decided to follow back to Greece the returning Achaian heroes of legend. He had previously visited the island of Ithaca (home of Odysseus) and Mycenae (citadel of Agamemnon) in 1868 before the start of his excavations at Troy. It was to Mycenae that he now returned, determined to find the burial places of Agamemnon and his followers, murdered when they came home victorious from Troy by Queen Clytemnestra and her lover Aegisthus. He began digging in 1874, sinking thirty-four trial trenches into the site, but was soon stopped by the authorities as he did not have the necessary permits.

Two years later, in August 1876, he began again, working with Stamatakis of the Greek Archaeological Service and concentrating his activities in four areas of the site. Two of the great stone-built tholos (round) tombs, known as the Treasury of Atreus and Tomb of Clytemnestra, which lay outside the city walls, caught his attention as Pausanias had described them as treasure houses: 'In the ruins of Mycenae is a water source called Perseia, and the underground chambers of Atreus and his sons where they kept the treasure-houses of their great wealth.' Small-scale excavations were also undertaken in the Lion Gate, but the main focus of Schliemann's search was for the graves of Agamemnon and his followers. Again he was guided by Pausanias, who wrote that these graves lay within the walls of the citadel, whereas those of Clytemnestra and Aegisthus lay outside. 'They were not fit to lie inside, where Agamemnon and the men murdered with him are lying.'

6. Schliemann's excavations in Grave Circle A at Mycenae in 1876.

Schliemann began digging inside the citadel walls, just to the south of the Lion Gate, on the right-hand side as you enter. Almost immediately he hit upon a stone circle and discovered within five fabulously rich graves, which he cleared in just twenty days. He then departed Mycenae, leaving the sixth and final grave in the circle to be found and excavated by Stamatakis. The contents of these graves amply justify the Homeric epithet for Mycenae: 'rich in gold'. Later scholarship was to show, though, that what Schliemann had found were not the burial places of Agamemnon and his followers, but rather those of much earlier rulers of Mycenae, buried there between around 1600 and 1450 BC. Nevertheless, with these extraordinary finds the discovery of the Mycenaeans was properly begun.

Hoping to repeat his spectacular successes at Troy and Mycenae, Schliemann went in search of Odysseus – eponymous hero of Homer's epic poem the *Odyssey* – and began excavations on the summit of Mount Aetos on the island of Ithaca, where he found the remains of houses but no great palace. After a second season at Troy in 1878–9 he returned to Greece, drawn to the site of Orchomenos in Boiotia by a Homeric reference to its great wealth: in the *Iliad* Achilles replies to Agamemnon's messenger that he would not return to the battlefield, 'not for all the riches of Orchomenos'. The great tholos tomb at

Orchomenos, then believed like those at Mycenae to be a treasure house, was well known. Pausanias had described it, still intact: 'The Treasure House of Minyas is one of the greatest wonders of Greece and of the world. It is built in stone, the shape is circular but the top does not stick up too sharply; they say the topmost stone is a keystone holding the entire building in place.' Schliemann began digging there in 1880–1, returning to the site in 1886. Given the fabled wealth of Orchomenos, Schliemann had high hopes of his excavations, but the going was extremely arduous as the corbelled stone ceiling had collapsed since Pausanias' day (as seen on Dodwell's drawing of the early nineteenth century; fig.3) and the large stones had first to be cleared. When this was done, the results were disappointing: no trace was found of the expected riches and the small side chamber contained little more than the fine carved slabs of greenish limestone that had once decorated the ceiling.[6]

7. Watercolour by William Simpson showing Mycenae in 1877. In the foreground are dumps from Schliemann's excavations.

Schliemann had missed the actual palace buildings at Mycenae (discovered later in 1886 on the summit of the hill by Christos Tsountas, a Greek archaeologist), so the first of the Mycenaean palaces to be excavated was that within the walls of Tiryns. The fortress of Tiryns, lying close to the coast not far from Mycenae in the Argive plain, had massive walls of hewn stone which earned it the Homeric epithet 'wall-girt'. Schliemann began to dig within the walls and, aided by W. Dörpfeld, found and excavated the palace between 1884–6.[7]

Schliemann died in 1890. Despite the controversy surrounding his methods, none can deny him the accolade that in his search to prove the historicity of the Homeric poems, he had discovered a lost civilization.

CHRONOLOGY

We now know that Schliemann found a level of the city of Troy that predated the legendary Trojan War and that the graves he unearthed at Mycenae were too early to have contained the burial of the legendary king Agamemnon. In the years since his discoveries, scholars have worked out a chronology for the Bronze Age Aegean. It is neither watertight nor foolproof and is constantly scrutinized, revised and refined in the face of new evidence and scientific methods, but it nevertheless provides us with a framework. With this framework in place we can begin to piece together the relative chronology of events in the Aegean and attempt to tie it in to real time and thus create an absolute chronology.[8]

8. The great walls of Tiryns.

The chronology that we have for the Bronze Age Aegean is a tripartite one that was originally devised for the Minoans on Crete by Arthur Evans, who divided the culture he found there into three parts – Early, Middle and Late Minoan. These same divisions were adopted for the Bronze Age on the Greek mainland, where they are called

Early, Middle and Late Helladic, and for the Cycladic culture of the islands. In terms of rough absolute dates these periods span the Bronze Age as follows: Early (3200–2000 BC), Middle (2000–1600 BC) and Late (1600–1100 BC). Each of these phases was then given three further subdivisions, which in their turn have been refined and divided. The use of this traditional tripartite system has become increasingly difficult to maintain as our understanding of the complexities of the Aegean Bronze Age has grown, and a variety of new systems and new terminologies have now been developed for different periods within the Bronze Age, especially for the earlier phases.

The relative chronology within this framework depends principally on the evolution of pottery styles, which are allotted an occasionally arbitrary number of years for the period during which they remained in use. There are few fixed points within the pottery sequences in the Aegean, but the eruption of Thera, placed at the end of Late Minoan Ia, is one of them. This relative chronology then has to be pinned at certain points to an absolute chronology, and for the Aegean Bronze Age this depends largely on synchronisms with Egypt and the Near East. Attempts at using science to provide absolute dates have produced controversial results, giving dates often strikingly at odds with those derived from the traditional synchronisms. This is particularly notable in the dates for the eruption of Thera: radiocarbon dates for the eruption, which would put it sometime in the seventeenth century BC rather than the traditionally derived date of around 1540 BC, run into problems with the Egyptian synchronisms.[9]

The Mycenaeans fit into the framework for the Bronze Age Aegean in the Late Bronze Age, their culture spanning the phase known as Late Helladic (the years around 1600 to 1100 BC). This is divided by scholars into Late Helladic (LH) I, II and III, with further subdivisions denoted by letters of the alphabet. In this book absolute dates will be given for ease of reading, but the relative chronology will sometimes be given in brackets afterwards.

The divisions of Late Helladic into I, II and III do not reflect any breaks in the archaeological record and thus the pottery styles of these three phases develop naturally out of each other. In essence, Mycenaean pottery evolved from the native Greek traditions of the Middle Bronze Age on the mainland and under artistic influence from the Minoans nearby on Crete. Throughout the centuries of the Mycenaeans we can trace a development of pottery shapes and decorative motifs, some of which die out at different times, while others continue and evolve. For this period we have fairly good synchronisms with Egypt and the Near East, which have enabled scholars to peg the relative chronology of developing pottery styles to the absolute chronology already established for those regions by written history. The short-lived capital of the heretic pharaoh Akhenaten at Tell el-Amarna on the Nile has, for instance, produced some 1600 sherds of Mycenaean pottery, which can thus be placed during the latter half of the fourteenth century BC. Attempts to radically modify the chronology for the Late Bronze Age by casting doubt on the absolute chronologies of Egypt and the Near East have been made, but have not been widely accepted.

The development of a chronological framework in which to place the Mycenaeans has allowed us to chart their progress across the years of the Late Bronze Age. It has also enabled us to evaluate where they stood in relation to the civilization of Greece in the historical period from which they were separated by the obscure centuries of the Dark Age. The Mycenaeans inhabited the same land as the later Greeks, but was there a closer connection? Were they themselves already Greek, or did Greek speakers enter the region after the end of the Bronze Age?

2

The Coming of the Greeks?

Heinrich Schliemann was convinced that the people whose tombs and palaces he had found on the Greek mainland were Homer's heroes: there was no doubt in his mind that they were Greek. Others, though, did not share his conviction. It was widely held that the Mycenaeans were a pre-Greek people and that they were displaced at the end of the Late Bronze Age by a wave of Greek-speaking newcomers, a phenomenon known as the Dorian Invasion. The discovery of large numbers of clay tablets inscribed with Linear B – the syllabic script of the Mycenaeans – and the subsequent decipherment of this script were finally to resolve the question of whether or not the Mycenaeans were Greeks.

LINEAR B

In 1939 an American archaeologist, Carl Blegen, dug his first trial trench into the hill of Ano Englianos in Messenia and discovered there not only the lost palace of the legendary king Nestor at Pylos, known from Homeric epic, but also the first evidence that the Mycenaeans had writing. He dug his trench right through what was later identified as the archive room of the palace and unearthed a cache of some 600 inscribed clay tablets, which detailed the workings of the palace bureaucracy. These were the first such tablets to be found on the Greek mainland and they were inscribed with a form of writing identical to that already discovered by Arthur Evans at Knossos in 1900.

Evans had identified two syllabic scripts while excavating the ruins of Minoan Crete, which he called Linear A and Linear B. He believed that the latter was a later script than the former, but that they were both used to write the same language, that of the Minoans. Neither of these scripts had been deciphered by the time of his death in 1941 and Linear A remains undeciphered to this day, with the language spoken by the Minoans yet to be identified.[1] The story of Linear B, however, found in far greater quantities than Linear A, has been rather different.

Linear B has since been found at other Mycenaean palaces – notably Mycenae, Tiryns and Thebes – but never in such quantities as at Knossos and Pylos. This script of the Mycenaean palaces is syllabic,

9. Linear B tablets found by Arthur Evans at Knossos: the upper one records offerings made to various deities and the lower one the number of sheep at Phaistos.
Below: Linear B ideograms.

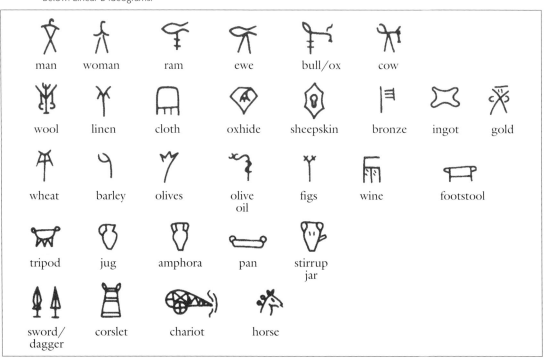

man	woman	ram	ewe	bull/ox	cow
wool	linen	cloth	oxhide	sheepskin	bronze	ingot	gold
wheat	barley	olives	olive oil	figs	wine	footstool
tripod	jug	amphora	pan	stirrup jar		
sword/ dagger	corslet	chariot	horse		

01	⊦	*da*	30	⅄	*ni*	59
02	✝	*ro*	31	⅄	*sa*	60
03	⧻	*pa*	32	⥍	*qo*	61
04	≢	*te*	33	⩓	*ra₃*	62
05	⊤	*to*	34	φ		63
06	⧖	*na*	35	φ		64
07	⊤⊤	*di*	36	⅁	*jo*	65
08	⊥	*a*	37	⋀	*ti*	66
09	⊩	*se*	38	A	*e*	67
10	f	*u*	39	Ⓐ	*pi*	68
11	⅂	*po*	40	⩕	*wi*	69
12	⅄	*so*	41	⅏	*si*	70
13	⅍	*me*	42	⋀³	*wo*	71
14	⅋	*do*	43	⅄	*ai*	72
15	⅌	*mo*	44	⋀⋀	*ke*	73
16	φ	*pa₂*	45	⋇	*de*	74
17	♀	*za*	46	⋈	*je*	75
18	⅄		47	⋇		76
19	⅍		48	⅄	*nwa*	77
20	⋔	*zo*	49	⌶		78
21	⥍	*qi*	50	⌂	*pu*	79
22	⋏		51	⧆	*du*	80
23	⅄	*mu*	52	⅏	*no*	81
24	⅄	*ne*	53	⅊	*ri*	82
25	⅄	*a₂*	54	⊞	*wa*	83
26	⅄	*ru*	55	⊡	*nu*	84
27	⅄	*re*	56	⊟	*pa₃*	85
28	⅄	*i*	57	⊟	*ja*	86
29	⅄	*pu₂*	58	⌐	*su*	87

59	*ta*
60	*ra*
61	*o*
62	*pte*
63	
64	
65	*ju*
66	*ta₂*
67	*ki*
68	*ro₂*
69	*tu*
70	*ko*
71	*dwe*
72	*pe*
73	*mi*
74	*ze*
75	*we*
76	*ra₂*
77	*ka*
78	*qe*
79	*zu*
80	*ma*
81	*ku*
82	
83	
84	
85	
86	
87	

10. Linear B signs.

with most of the signs representing not a letter as in our own alphabet, but a syllable. It also uses a complex system of numbering and has many ideograms: schematic representations of such things as men and women, animals, weapons and armour, vessels and foods. The various signs were inscribed onto damp clay tablets of two basic forms, rectangular page-shaped and smaller leaf-shaped, which were then sun-dried and kept as the yearly records of the economic activity of the palaces.

Linear B was deciphered by a brilliant and dedicated young architect, Michael Ventris, later joined in his research by the Cambridge philologist John Chadwick. His work proved that although the script appears to have developed out of the earlier Minoan Linear A it was actually used to write an entirely different language. In June 1952, on a radio programme, Ventris made the following momentous announcement: 'During the last few weeks, I have come to the conclusion that the Knossos and Pylos tablets must, after all, be written in Greek – a difficult and archaic Greek seeing that it is 500 years older than Homer and written in a rather abbreviated form, but Greek nevertheless.'

Ventris's great discovery was that Greek, or rather a very early form of it that evolved over time into the language of Homer and the later Classical Greek writers, had been spoken by the Mycenaeans, and that they were, as Schliemann had always maintained, the forebears of the Classical Greeks.

ARRIVALS OF NEWCOMERS IN THE BRONZE AGE?

The realization that an early form of Greek was already spoken by the Mycenaeans revolutionized scholarly thinking on the question of the 'coming of the Greeks'. The search for when proto-Greek speakers first arrived was provoked by a tradition preserved in Classical Greek literature that there had been a time in the distant past when a language or languages other than Greek had been spoken in the land. Thucydides wrote in the fifth century BC that 'Hellas' (Greece) had once been home to different tribes, with the Pelasgians being the strongest. Herodotus elaborates on this, telling us that the Dorians were a Hellenic people who spoke Greek, whereas the Ionians were an indigenous race of Pelasgians who spoke a non-Greek language. Strabo records the words of the Ionian historian Hekatios the Milesian, who said that before the Greeks arrived the country was inhabited by 'barbaroi' (barbarians), the term used by the Greeks for all those who spoke a foreign tongue. Philologists have found some evidence in the language itself to support this tradition. Greek belongs to the Indo-European family of languages, but it incorporates some words – usually proper names – which are distinctly non-Indo-European in origin. Words incorporating -nth- (Korinthos) and -ss-\-s-\-z- (Parnassos) are seen as remnants of one or more non-Greek languages.

Attempts have therefore been made to identify the 'coming of the Greeks' in the archaeological record by looking for breaks in cultural continuity: the arrival of new people, bringing with them different forms of pottery, weapons and tomb types and using new technologies. Any such incursions would have to have been on a large enough scale to supplant the language spoken by the previous inhabitants.

Could the Mycenaeans themselves have been newcomers, bringing an early form of Greek with them? Dramatic changes in terms of wealth are certainly demonstrated by the contents of the graves of Circle A at Mycenae, but when looked at with Circle B (see Chapter 3) it is clear that the culture of the Late Bronze Age Mycenaeans grew out of that of the preceding Middle Bronze Age period, with no evidence for large-scale incursions of new peoples. A study of the centuries of the Middle Bronze Age (2000–1600 BC) has likewise drawn a blank.

Going yet further back, the search for disruption and radical change focused on the Early Bronze Age in Greece (3200–2000 BC). The beginnings of this period were firmly anchored in the preceding Neolithic, with the people living in small settlements rather isolated from one another. Towards the middle of it, though, there was a rise both in the population and in the numbers of settlements, some of which were fortified, and there are clear signs of contact between various regions, in marked contrast to the preceding phase.

This incipient burgeoning of society came to a violent end around 2300 BC. At Lerna in the Argolid – a strongly fortified site with well-built houses and an imposing structure known as the House of Tiles – traces of burning were found everywhere.[2] This pattern is echoed elsewhere at the same time: Ayios Kosmas, Zygouries, Asine and Tiryns all suffered violent destructions in 2300 BC, at the end of what is known as Early Helladic II. It is also clear that at Lerna, following the destruction, the character of the settlement changed dramatically, with new house forms, pottery types and tool types indicating different technologies. Some of these changes can also be seen at other sites, such as Manika and Lefkandi on the island of Euboia, Kolonna on Aigina, and on the island of Kea. Thus around this time we find the most convincing break in the archaeological record. Widespread violent destructions of an established way of life were followed at some sites by what may be the arrival of new people bringing with them their own objects and technology. The closest parallels for the material culture of these new people are to be found in Anatolia (modern Turkey).

Can this then be the 'coming of the Greeks'? If we are to look, as traditional scholarship has done, for a single break, then this might well be our best candidate. However, more recent thinking tends to the view that it is too simplistic to think in terms of a single wave of Greek-speakers sweeping into the area. It is possible, for instance, that from very early times several languages were spoken in the region, with Greek gradually becoming dominant and winning out in the end. It

11. View of Lerna in the Argolid.

was not, after all, until after the end of the Bronze Age that Greek took over on Crete from the as yet unidentified language spoken by the Minoans.

Whatever the significance of the destructions of c.2300 BC for the vexed question of the 'coming of the Greeks', what is certain is that they severely disrupted the pace of social development seen in the preceding centuries, and the incipient sophistication of that society was lost. Greece reverted to the poverty, regionalism and isolationism that had characterized its settlements and the lives of its people at the start of the Early Bronze Age. It was not really to recover until the late years of the Middle Bronze Age, when, in the seventeenth century BC, we again see the beginnings of a more complex and wealthy society, one that was to develop into the Late Bronze Age culture of the Mycenaeans.

THE MIDDLE BRONZE AGE GREEKS

For much of the Middle Bronze Age (2000–1600 BC), the mainland of Greece was a cultural backwater, particularly when viewed in comparison with Crete, where the Minoans had established a sophisticated and outward-looking palace culture.

The Middle Bronze Age forebears of the Mycenaeans led simple lives: they lived off the land and used local resources wherever possible, only importing raw materials when absolutely necessary.[5] The communities lived in small villages, some of which were fortified, especially towards the end of the period. Their homes were built from easily accessible local resources and had mud-brick walls, sometimes supported by a timber frame built on stone foundations. Although there was some variety in the shape of the houses, which were basically rectangular but could have an apsidal (rounded) end, they didn't vary much in size, showing that there was little social stratification. In some instances, though, larger buildings have been found, such as the so-called 'palace' at Marathon and a megaron (large hall) at Thebes, which may indicate some form of social hierarchy.

Many of the inhabitants of these small villages were farmers, but some of them must also have had specialist skills as the community

12. Middle Bronze Age Grey Minyan Ware goblet and two-handled cups; their sharply carinated shapes are probably derived from metal prototypes.

would have needed the expertise of craftworkers like builders, metal-workers and potters.

Pottery was clearly an important commodity and the closest we come to a form of writing at this time is in the marks made by potters on their products. Two kinds of pottery were made: matt-painted, with dark linear abstract patterns added to a buff ground; and Minyan, which is usually grey, but is also found in yellow, red and black. Minyan Ware is characterized by its soft, soapy texture and its sharply carinated shapes, which may indicate metal prototypes. It derives its title from Schliemann, who first identified it at Orchomenos in Boiotia and named it after the legendary dynasty of the Minyans who were said to have ruled there. Craftsmen using other locally available raw materials were clearly making products in a workshop in a house at Eutresis, which contained quantities of bone, boar's tusk and mother of pearl. Metalworking is seen at some sites, with copper-working at Nichoria and silver-smelting at Thorikos. Metals seem to have been in short supply, but silver, lead and probably copper were apparently mined locally at Laurion in Attica. Some other vital raw materials also had to be acquired from outside the immediate vicinity of the village. Obsidian (a very hard volcanic material) was often used to make tools and weapons like arrowheads and axes. The Cycladic island of Melos was the nearest source of obsidian, used in Greece since Mesolithic times: long before the island was inhabited, people were visiting it to collect supplies.

The paths of trading networks supplying raw materials like metals and obsidian to the communities of the Middle Bronze Age can be traced by the scatters of pottery left in their wake. In the early years of the Middle Bronze Age these trading networks seem to have linked the mainland of Greece with the Cycladic islands and with the island of Aigina. Some of the settlements – such as Lerna in the Argolid, Ayios Stephanos in the south of the Peloponnese, and Kolonna on Aigina – seem to have been particularly involved in this. Crete at this stage seems to have had a relatively unimportant role in trade with the mainland, though the Minoans did apparently trade for lead, silver and possibly copper from Laurion. Some Minoan pottery has been found on the mainland, but is probably more likely to have come from the Minoan settlement of Kastri on the island Kythera, or perhaps from the less-well-developed regions of western Crete, rather than the major palace centres. Trading networks were also operating in the north of Greece, with mainland pottery and imported Cycladic and Minoan wares reaching the site of Peukakia, near Volos in Thessaly.

The simple life led by the Greeks of the Middle Bronze Age is reflected in their burials: in death, as in life, they left little that was spectacular until the period drew to a close in the seventeenth century BC. Their graves, though, paint for us a picture of a society with strong cultural uniformity, with similar forms of burial seen over great stretches of the mainland. Adults, both male and female, were mostly placed as a single burial in a simple dug-out pit or in a cist grave built of slabs of stone. Sometimes adults were buried inside large clay *pithoi* (storage jars), though these were more commonly used for the bodies of children. Multiple burials were usually made in a tumulus: a large mound of earth heaped above a number of pit or cist burials, sometimes with a central grave at the heart of the mound. Some of these tumuli were very impressive burial monuments, measuring up to 25 m (82 ft) in diameter.

Children tended to be buried within the confines of the village, often under the floors of the houses themselves. Adult burials have also been discovered within settlements, utilizing abandoned houses and often incorporating house walls in the structure of the grave. In general, though, adult graves are found in groups outside the settlement: in small clusters next to it; or in subdivided burial plots in larger cemeteries either adjacent to it or further afield in the countryside; or in grave circles or tumuli. The groups probably reflect families, maintaining kinship ties in death as in life.

The bodies are usually found lying on their side in a contracted position, many buried with no grave goods at all and those that are with few and simple offerings. Clay vases were the most common gift to the dead, especially vessels associated with drinking and eating, such as cups, jugs and bowls. Children were occasionally given a feeding bottle, perhaps one they had used when alive, or miniature vessels, made especially as scaled-down offerings. Basic ornaments were sometimes placed with the dead, such as simple jewellery of shells or stone beads, and the occasional weapon or tool of bronze, obsidian or flint. Animal offerings were also made, in some cases as food for the dead and in others as the sacrifice of a valued personal possession, such as a dog or horse.

Against this uniform background, a handful of burials stand out: most notable amongst them are the warrior burials, precursors of those of the Mycenaean period. A cist grave at Thebes contained the burial of a warrior accompanied by a sword, spear, boar's-tusk helmet (the high-status helmet of later Mycenaean warriors) and arrows. Likewise, at the main gate of the fortification wall at Kolonna on Aigina, lying in a large cist grave, a warrior was found wearing a gold diadem and equipped with a fine set of weapons (a long sword, spear and obsidian arrowheads). Also in his tomb were placed a boar's-tusk helmet, a bronze razor and pottery, both local and imported.

Even the humblest of burials, though, may tell us something of the lives of those who lie there if the remains are discovered in a reasonable state of preservation. A study of skeletons found at Lerna in the Argolid has shown that the people who lived there were of very mixed racial stock, muscular and strong in build but suffering from a number of health problems, such as malnutrition in childhood, bad teeth, arthritis and malaria. This is probably largely typical of the region as a whole in the Middle Bronze Age, though the malaria is likely to have been specific to Lerna and caused by the very swampy conditions at the settlement. The men were about 1.60–1.70 m (5 ft 2 in–5ft 6 in) tall and lived to around thirty to forty-five years old, whereas the women were usually between 1.48–1.56 m (4 ft 10 in–5 ft 1 in) tall and had rather shorter lives, with an average lifespan of twenty-five to forty years.

Towards the end of the Middle Bronze Age changes were clearly afoot on the mainland of Greece: an increase in the number of settlements implies a rise in the population; and there is more diversity and experimentation in burial types and a growth in the wealth and variety of the grave goods. This increasing prosperity and confidence at home is reflected in greater contact with the outside world, most notably with the sophisticated and outward-looking palace culture that had been established by the Minoans on Crete in the early years of the Middle Bronze Age (c.2000 BC).[3]

These signs of incipient prosperity and cosmopolitanism which mark the final years of the Middle Bronze Age are perhaps most clearly seen in the burials of Grave Circle B, the earlier of the two great Grave Circles at Mycenae. Here, within this Circle, we see the Middle Bronze Age end and the Late Bronze Age begin.

3

The Grave Circles of Mycenae

When Schliemann excavated Grave Circle A within the walls of Mycenae he uncovered burials which stood at the very beginning of the Late Bronze Age culture of Greece, the culture we now call Mycenaean. These graves, dating to between 1600 and 1450 BC, contained a wealth of riches which appeared as a sudden splash of brilliance against the relative poverty that had characterized much of the Middle Bronze Age. The graves of Circle B, discovered subsequently, bridged the gap between the Middle and Late Bronze Ages, the earlier burials belonging to the former and the later ones the latter. The discovery that there were two Grave Circles at Mycenae, for at least part of their history running concurrently, immediately led to speculation that they reflected a tradition of dual kingship, with two ruling families using separate burial places. This was seen by some as confirmation from the site of the legends that surround it, namely that Atreus and Thyestes – two sons of Pelops and Hippodameia – competed for the throne of Mycenae.

The rectangular shaft graves of Circles A and B have given their name to the first one hundred and fifty years of Mycenaean culture: the Shaft Grave Era – a time when much of our evidence for the early Mycenaeans comes not from settlement sites but from burials. Settlement evidence is sparse in this period, partly from later building over earlier remains, and partly because it appears that the Mycenaeans of the Shaft Grave Era invested much of their wealth in funerary display rather than in their living quarters. Some of the gold objects found in the graves, such as diadems, stars, shroud ornaments and some vessels, were far too fragile to have been used in life and must have been made specially for the funeral and the tomb. The bodies of men, women and children were elaborately dressed for their funeral – particularly those buried in Grave Circle A – and must have looked extraordinarily impressive. Men were laid out in gold masks and funerary armour, women in high gold crowns, their clothes gleaming with gold ornaments, and children were wrapped from head to toe in sheet gold. Together, the dress, adornments and other funerary goods, some made specially for the burial and others personal items used in life, not only reflect the status of the dead but also reveal their personalities.

GRAVE CIRCLE B

Grave Circle B was discovered in 1951 when workmen digging close to the tholos tomb known as the Tomb of Clytemnestra – lifting earth to cover over its newly restored roof – came across a sculptured stone stele, similar to those Schliemann had found above the graves of Circle A in 1876. Excavations began in July 1952 under the direction of I. Papadimitriou and G. Mylonas, and were continued over the next two years.[1]

Grave Circle B lies outside the citadel walls of Mycenae on slightly raised ground, some 117 m (338 ft) from the Lion Gate. Its low rubble circuit wall, with a diameter of 28 m (91 ft), is partially preserved and its construction is very similar to the original one of Circle A. Twenty-six graves were excavated within Circle B: most were shaft graves, with grave stelai standing over four of them, and a few were simple pit burials. The shaft graves in Circle B were assigned letters of the Greek alphabet to distinguish them from those of Circle A. Most of the graves were oriented north-south but a few were east-west, and men and women were sometimes buried in separate graves and sometimes together. Whereas Circle A was subsequently incorporated within the walls of the citadel of Mycenae when the fortified area was increased, Circle B was left outside and not accorded the same respect. It was encroached on by later tombs: Grave Rho was subsequently re-used and adapted into a monumental built tomb and the Tomb of Clytemnestra was constructed perilously close. This may indicate that the families buried in Circle A became dominant in early Mycenaean society and were therefore revered by successive rulers at the site.

Despite this later damage, and the fact that even during the use of the Circle later tombs were sometimes dug into earlier ones, the graves were found for the most part intact. It was possible therefore to study the position and treatment of the bodies in the tomb and to record with accuracy the deposition of the grave goods. Where multiple burials took place, earlier occupants of the tomb were cleared to one side and their grave goods piled up with them, so it was sometimes only possible to identify the original position of those goods laid in the grave for the final burial. In total, the twenty-six graves enclosed in Grave Circle B contained the burials of thirty-five people – men, women and children.

The first burials dug within Grave Circle B belong to the Middle Bronze Age and the latest to the beginnings of the Late Bronze Age, the early Mycenaean period. The Middle Bronze Age graves were characteristically small and shallow with few and poor grave goods, usually consisting of pottery vessels – the most popular shape being a *kylix* (stemmed goblet) – and the occasional weapon. Gradually the graves dug in the Circle grew larger and the goods deposited within them correspondingly richer, more numerous and more varied. This

13. Rock-crystal vessel in the form of a duck from Grave Omicron, Circle B.

diversification is seen in burials like Grave Beta, which held a man equipped with a dagger, an amulet of gold and a strip of electrum; the earliest instance of precious metal ornaments in the Circle. Grave Iota similarly exhibited a growing range of grave goods, including gold shroud ornaments, gold cuff-trimmings, amber beads and bone objects. The shaft grave burials of this middle phase see the beginnings of the funerary display that was to culminate in the richest burials of Circle A.

In its final phase of use, the latest graves of Circle B (Alpha, Gamma, Delta, Epsilon, Nu and Omicron) – contemporary with the earliest of Circle A in the sixteenth century BC – were dug into the north and the centre of the Circle. The majority of the pottery vessels found in them were in traditional mainland fabrics and styles, but some were imports from the Cycladic islands and others reflected the growing influence of Minoan Crete on the culture of the mainland. All the tombs contained a rich variety of grave offerings, including some exceptionally beautiful individual objects, but none to rival the richest of Circle A.

The identities of those buried in the graves begin to emerge with the different kinds of grave goods found with them. That the men who lay in these later graves of Circle B were warriors is evident: their clothing trimmed with gold, they were interred with many weapons, such as swords, daggers, spears and knives. The piles of broken or damaged bronze swords probably reflected their prowess in battle and in the hunt, while more ornamental weapons, such as a dagger blade inlaid with a strip of electrum (Grave Nu), or a sword with an ivory pommel (Grave Delta), were more likely to have been for ceremonial use only.

Some of the women in the graves were clearly wealthy and important members of the ruling élite of Mycenae, placed in the tomb richly dressed and accompanied by fine jewellery and personal items. A woman in Grave Upsilon was buried wearing a crown of bronze with gold leaves, a gold hair-ring, silver earrings and a double necklace of gold and silver beads. Another in Grave Omicron had a diadem of gold bands, necklaces of gold flying birds, amber, cornelian and amethyst. Attached to her funerary garment were three bronze pins with rock-crystal heads, a silver pin and a large gold-leaf rosette. Also from this grave came a beautiful little cosmetic bowl of rock crystal in the form of a duck.

Skeletal remains from Circle B

The skeletal remains from the graves in Circle B were found in a good state of preservation and have since been intensively examined by forensic scientists. Of the thirty-five people buried there, twenty-two have been studied: sixteen men, four women and two children. Their skeletons reveal that they were at the top of the physical range, as one might expect of a ruling élite. They were taller and more strongly built than the people of Lerna, for instance, though of the same mixed racial stock. The men had an average height of c.1.71 m (5 ft 7 in) and the women of c.1.59 m (5 ft 2 in), some 6 cm (2 in) taller than the Middle Bronze Age people of Lerna. They lived to an average age of thirty-eight years and were healthy, with a good diet and strong teeth. The men were robustly built, strong and muscular, with large hands and feet; the women were also strong and robust. Of the two children studied, one had died aged two and the other aged five.

Many of the male skeletons from these graves showed signs of injury, probably received in battle. One of them had undergone trepanning (a surgical procedure in which a hole is made in the skull in an attempt to relieve pressure from a head injury) and another had a healed fracture of his spinal column. Others showed deformations of the skeleton, probably caused by years of fighting, such as a lump on the shoulder bone, which was perhaps from carrying a heavy shield slung over the shoulder. In general, though, they were in good health, with few signs of infections or diet-related illnesses, though one did have gallstones. Interestingly, it is clear that their diet included very few marine foods, and was almost exclusively one of various types of meat and vegetables.

Forensic scientists have also undertaken facial reconstructions of some of the people in the tombs to see what they would have looked like in life.[2] Before this work was undertaken, our image of these early Mycenaean warriors depended on two artefacts from Grave Gamma which gave us representations of male faces. One was an exquisitely carved amethyst seal showing a male head in profile with long hair and beard, which was once thought to depict a Mycenaean but is now believed to be a Minoan priest. The other was a death mask made of electrum, but found in a wooden box and not placed over the face as those in Grave Circle A had been. The mask has a triangular-shaped face, high forehead and small features, all of which can be seen in the

14. Electrum mask from Grave Gamma, Circle B.

subsequent reconstruction of the actual head of its owner, but it was not in any true sense a real portrait.

The reconstruction work undertaken on some of the best-preserved skulls from Circle B has revealed a few of the faces of the men and women in the graves. It has also allowed us to trace family resemblances and thus to try to establish family groups within the Circle.

Of the four women studied, only one had a skull in a state of preservation that would allow such a reconstruction to be made, and even in this case part of the front of the skull was missing. This woman was buried in Grave Gamma, her remains swept to the side of the tomb to allow for a subsequent burial. She was tall (1.60 m [5 ft 2 in]) and strong, yet of fairly slender build, and had died in her mid-thirties, already showing signs of arthritis in her back and hands. Her right arm had been broken, but had mended well. When reconstructed, her face was heart-shaped with a pronounced forehead, strong jaw and small widely spaced eyes. Her hairstyle – with a pony tail and long loose

15. Reconstruction from a woman's skull from Grave Gamma, Circle B.

tresses of hair – is conjectural, but based on fashions for mature women seen on later fresco paintings.

The skulls of the males were in far better condition, and facial reconstructions have been made of several of them. One of the most imposing in appearance was a man from Grave Sigma, standing about 1.75 m (5 ft 8 in) tall and aged about fifty when he died. He was clearly a great warrior in his time, his skeletal remains showing signs of many injuries, such as blows to his head, fractured ribs (presumably sustained in battle or the hunt) and deformed shoulder blades from

16. Reconstruction from a warrior's skull from Grave Sigma, Circle B.

carrying a heavy shield. The reconstruction of his skull showed him to have had a narrow high forehead, small closely set eyes, narrow nose and strong jaw; the hairstyle and beard are again conjectural, derived from the so-called 'Mask of Agamemnon' from Grave Circle A.

Family resemblances have been traced within the clusters of tombs in Grave Circle B and, as one might expect, skulls from within the same grave or groups of graves do resemble each other, while those from different areas of the Circle do not, with occasional notable exceptions (for example, one individual from Grave Zeta appears to have a family resemblance to one from Grave Gamma).

GRAVE CIRCLE A

The six graves of Circle A had initially been surrounded by a low circular rubble wall and lay beyond the boundaries of the settlement on the acropolis. In the middle of the thirteenth century BC an extension to the citadel walls had been built in such a way as to encompass the graves within the fortifications. It was at this stage that Grave Circle A was given the form in which it was excavated by Schliemann and as we see it today. Upright limestone slabs were erected in a double row around the perimeter of the Circle and other slabs were set horizontally above them to form a continuous circular bench. The diameter of this stone circle was 27.5 m (almost 90 ft) and it had one entrance, near to the Lion Gate. The area of this circle within the acropolis of Mycenae was never built over during the subsequent history of the city, and tradition preserved the memory that it was a burial place; thus Pausanias was told that Agamemnon lay buried within the walls of Mycenae when he visited so many centuries later.

The shaft graves within Circle A – excavated by Schliemann and by Stamatakis of the Greek Archaeological Service in 1876 – date to the first 150 years of Mycenaean culture, from around 1600 to 1450 BC (LHI and IIA).[3] All but one of them contained multiple burials of between two and five people, giving a total of nineteen bodies: nine men, eight women and two children. As in Circle B, some graves were reserved for either men or women and some were mixed.

Limestone stelai marked the graves: six of them plain and eleven carved in relief with abstract curvilinear patterns and figured scenes, which reflect the Mycenaeans' obvious enthusiasm for warfare and hunting. One particularly fine gravestone shows a horse-drawn chariot carrying a warrior holding a dagger or sword, the horses' hooves trampling a warrior with a figure-of-eight shield; whilst in the scene below, a lion pursues a goat or deer. Another shows a chariot drawn by a galloping horse, the warrior within brandishing a weapon and faced by a warrior on foot, either armed with or transfixed by a spear. These finely sculpted stelai reflect the warlike character of the early rulers of Mycenae, and the contents of the graves they marked were to bear further witness to it.

The graves lay some 8 m (26 ft) down, 5 m (16 ft) of which were below the level of the rock. The graves themselves were large rectangular shafts (hence the name 'shaft graves') cut into the earth and soft rock of the Mycenae acropolis, their walls lined with rubble. The dead were laid – usually with their heads to the east and feet to the west, accompanied by rich grave goods – in the rectangular chamber of the tomb on a floor of small pebbles. Across ledges, formed by the top of the rubble lining walls, wooden beams were set, which in turn supported a roof of twigs and branches covered over by a layer of clay and stone slabs. The hole in the ground above the tomb was then filled in

17. Grave stele from Circle A, decorated with spirals and a chariot scene.

18. Gold death masks from Circle A.

with earth and it had to be reopened for subsequent burials. Although the shaft grave appears at first to be an entirely new kind of tomb, it is in fact a development in more sophisticated form of the Middle Bronze Age cist grave.

The élite who buried their dead here lavished extraordinary riches upon them, and in doing so left clues as to the nature of this early Mycenaean society, its wealth and its links with the wider world. It was clearly important that the funerals of the ruling family members were conspicuous in their splendour and display, and many items made of thin sheet gold, too fragile for everyday use, were placed in the graves. However, personal possessions, such as tweezers, tools, knives, and pottery vessels, were probably included for the use of the dead in the afterlife.

Male burials

The bodies of the warriors in Circle A must have looked fearsome and impressive when laid out in all their glory for the funeral. Such an exhibition of affluence and power can surely not have been intended just for the tomb or for the benefit of close family members: the body must have been placed on public view as it lay laden with gold and surrounded by weapons and fabulous and exotic offerings. Necklaces, often of amber beads, were hung around the neck and the funerary clothes were ornamented with gold trim and buttons.

The five warriors who were buried wearing gold death masks – three in Grave IV and two in Grave V – must have looked particularly imposing, especially when they also wore a breastplate of sheet gold. One of the men in Grave IV was adorned with a gold breastplate and a mask of exceptionally thick sheet gold, depicting the face of a man with a large forehead and a wide thin-lipped mouth. Two warriors from the same grave were also wearing masks, which, though recognizably individual, shared certain facial characteristics, with the same small mouth and heavy eyebrows meeting across the bridge of a long straight nose. These similarities in the masks may reflect a family resemblance or simply arise from both the masks being made by the same craftsman or workshop following similar conventions for the portrayal of the human face. Unfortunately, the majority of the skulls

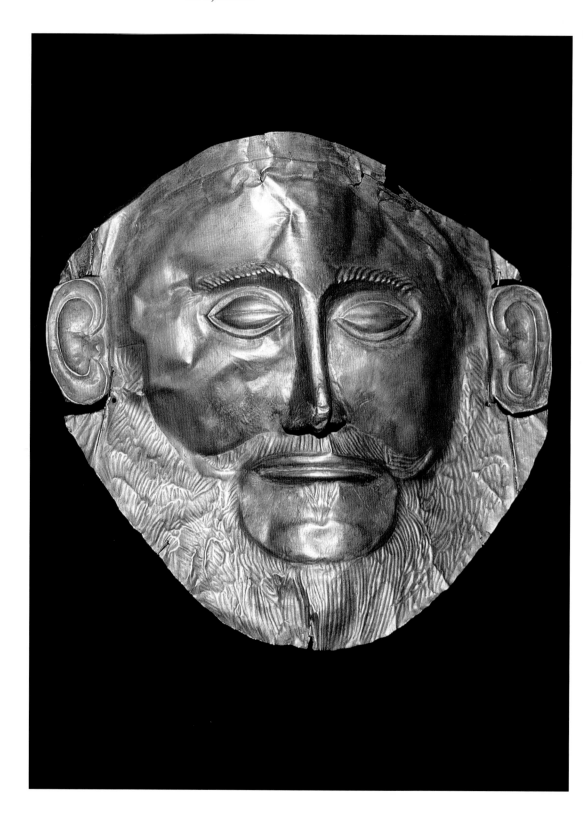

found in the tombs of Circle A were in a much poorer state of preservation than those of Circle B, and so the question cannot be answered by facial reconstruction.

Of the masked warriors in Grave V, one wore a splendid gold breastplate decorated with spirals, and a gold mask depicting a bearded face with a moustache and an aquiline nose. This mask has become known as the 'Mask of Agamemnon' and it certainly is the most aristocratic of the five in appearance. However, it was another masked warrior from the same grave that Schliemann believed to be the great king. Over his face lay a heavy gold mask with a round face, exceptionally large forehead and small mouth. When it was lifted off, Schliemann was surprised by the extraordinary state of preservation of the face below:

> Of the third body, which lay at the north end of the tomb, the round face, with all its flesh, had been wonderfully preserved under its ponderous gold mask; there was no vestige of hair, but both eyes were perfectly visible, also the mouth, which owing to the enormous weight that had been pressed upon it, was wide open, and showed thirty-two beautiful teeth...

The body thus preserved lay flattened to a thickness of between 2 and 5 cm (c.1–2 in), crushed by the weight of earth pressing upon it from above where the roof of the tomb had collapsed.

This body has become known as the 'shaft grave mummy'. Schliemann himself wrote, 'The colour of the body resembled very much that of an Egyptian mummy', but it was only after it was subsequently preserved that he called it 'the now nearly mummified body'. Schliemann, fearing its immediate disintegration, commissioned an oil painting, but in the event it lasted for two days – long enough for someone to come from Athens to preserve it with gum-sandarac dissolved in alcohol. The then-solidified body was cut out of the grave in a shallow slab and sent to Athens. It has been suggested that this was not the body of a Mycenaean warrior king but rather that of an Egyptian princess, married to a Mycenaean and embalmed according to the custom of her own people. However, the grave goods show that it was a male; none of the women in the shaft graves was buried with swords or death masks. The mystery of how this body came to be so well preserved in the tomb has yet to be solved. A study of the 'mummy' is planned and forensic science may answer some of the questions it poses.

Large quantities of weapons, both functional and ornamental, were found lying beside the bodies of the men in the tombs. Of these, the many broken and damaged swords (also seen in Circle B) may have been those used by the warrior during his lifetime and placed with him in death as a testimony to his power. Bronze spearheads and obsidian

19. The 'Mask of Agamemnon' from Grave V, Circle A.

20. Oil painting of the 'shaft grave mummy' from Grave V, Circle A.

arrowheads were also placed in the tombs, as were more unusual weapons like tridents and battleaxes.

A number of the weapons were elaborately made and probably used for ceremonial occasions rather than in battle. The wooden hilts of some swords were gold-plated or decorated with gold discs – with one particularly fine example executed in *cloisonné* – whilst others had ivory or marble pommels. The bronze blades of some of the weapons were decorated in relief with rows of horses, griffins and figure-of-eight shields. Finest of all were the daggers found in Graves IV and V, their blades inlaid with miniature scenes in precious metals. One from Grave IV depicts in exquisite detail a scene of Mycenaean warriors hunting lions. The hunters wear short kilts and carry long hunting spears and large body shields of two types: the figure-of-eight shield and a large rectangular one known as a tower shield. One hunter lies prostrate on the ground below the paws of an oncoming lion and another, an archer, draws his bow. Towards the tip, two more lions are depicted in flight. The other side of the blade shows a lion hunting antelope, a juxtaposition of hunter and prey much favoured by the Mycenaeans. The lion was symbolic of great strength and was a suitable quarry for Mycenaean warriors, who may well have hunted the animal in areas of Greece in the Bronze Age. The hunting theme is continued on a dagger from Grave V, which is decorated on both sides with a spotted wild cat stalking ducks by the side of a river set in a Nilotic landscape. The flora and fauna of the scene are derived from the Nile. The obvious Egyptian influence was probably introduced via Minoan Crete, which had close ties with Pharaonic Egypt at this time.

The only defensive armour that survived in the graves were the gold breastplates (of thin sheet gold and therefore presumably ornamental) and pieces of carved boar's tusk, the remains of boar's-tusk helmets. These helmets were made of a felt-lined leather cap clad with rows of cut boar's tusk. They have been found in Mycenaean warrior

21. Dagger inlaid with a scene of men hunting lions from Grave IV, Circle A.

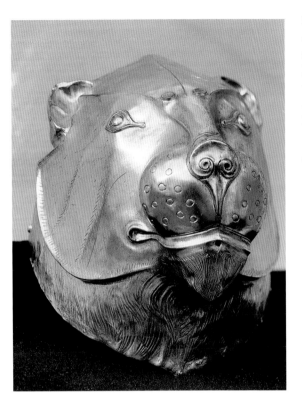

22. Gold *rhyton* in the shape of a lion's head from Grave IV, Circle A.

burials throughout the Late Bronze Age and are seen worn by warriors on frescoes, seal-stones and ivory carvings. The boar's-tusk helmet must have been greatly prized and was a high-status piece of armour as it took around sixty boars' tusks to make just one helmet.

Cups, stemmed goblets and jugs in gold, silver and electrum – many of them extremely ornate – were found in quantities in the tombs, as were large cooking vessels of bronze, often showing signs of use. Such vessels would have been used by the Mycenaeans while feasting and drinking and perhaps also during rituals and ceremonies. Clearly for ceremonial use were the *rhyta* (ritual sprinkling vessels) found in Grave IV, made of precious materials and in their variety illustrating a range of contacts and influences. One example, a *rhyton* in the form of a lion's head made of thick sheet gold, looks like the product of a Mycenaean craftsman; another, a silver bull's head with gilded horns, clearly follows Minoan prototypes; whilst a third, a silver stag *rhyton*, must be a rare import from the Hittite civilization of Anatolia. A silver conical *rhyton* from the same grave, found in a very fragmentary condition, was intricately decorated in *repoussé* with scenes of warriors laying siege to a city that vividly evokes Homer's descriptions of the siege of Troy. The largest preserved fragment shows a coastal plain and a city on a hill; another, olive trees growing beside a city in which women in Minoan dress stand watching the battle raging below them.

Female burials

The wealth deposited in the graves with the women of Mycenae shows that some of them at least had a high status in the community. They must have belonged to the families of the ruling élite and although the offerings for them were different in character from those of the men, they were just as rich.

The opulence of the women's funerary ensemble is most evident in Grave III, which held the bodies of three women and two children. The women were not buried wearing death masks, but rather gold diadems, the finest of them a large crown decorated in *repoussé* with rosettes and circles and with leaves of sheet gold attached to wires that stood up from its upper edge. Six more gold diadems, decorated with bosses and spirals, were also found in the tomb. The women were

23. Large gold crown decorated with bosses from a women's grave in Circle A.

laden with jewellery, which perhaps represented what they owned in life. They had several pairs of gold earrings and many necklaces, pendant pomegranates being among the finest of the gold beads. Their funerary clothing, presumably of very fine textiles that have not survived, was sewn or stuck all over with elaborate gold ornaments. Some of the shroud ornaments were circular discs decorated in *repoussé* with octopuses, cuttlefish, butterflies, flowers, spirals and leaves, whilst others were cut-outs of butterflies, griffins, a swimming octopus and lions attacking a bull. Small ornaments in the form of a naked goddess holding her hands to her breasts, accompanied by doves and birds of prey, and of tripartite shrines surmounted by horns of consecration and perching birds reflect the influence of Minoan religious iconography. Pins were used to hold the funerary garment in place, the most elaborate of them made of a heavy silver shaft and a gold head in the form of a bare-breasted woman wearing a long flounced skirt and with palm branches cascading from volutes and papyrus flowers on top of her head. Precious personal items had also been placed in the tomb with the women, including gold seals and a gold comb with bone teeth, as had other rich offerings such as a faience *rhyton* in the form of a triton shell and several gold and silver cups and jugs.

Children

Infant mortality was very high and the death of a baby or child must have been commonplace. It is therefore clear that the two children buried with the three women in Grave III were of great importance. At least one of them had their tiny body wrapped in sheet gold from head to toe, with a mask for the face. The small gold hands and feet of the suit still keep the shape of the fingers and toes, one hand holding a ring of thin gold wire. The tiny bones have not survived in the tomb, so it

24. Sheet gold wrappings for a child buried in Circle A.

is not possible to say if the two were girls or boys, and the mask gives little away, consisting of a little mask for the eyes and strips for the lower face.

Cult of the dead?

When Schliemann excavated Grave Circle A he found a circular mass of stones that he believed to be an altar at which the living made offerings to the dead. The structure is now lost and it is therefore difficult to evaluate this idea, but no other evidence has been found at the Circle to indicate such a cult. However, the respect in which the Grave Circle was held by subsequent generations of Mycenaeans is demonstrated by the special provisions made in the restructuring of the citadel in the thirteenth century to incorporate it within the protective orbit of the citadel walls.

The ruling élite who buried their dead in Grave Circle A did so with an ostentatious display of wealth that was aimed at defining and reinforcing their power and authority over the people of Mycenae. Looking beyond the confines of Mycenae itself we can see that a similar process appears to have been in operation elsewhere on the mainland at the same time, though apparently not on such a lavish scale.

4

The Shaft Grave Era

The first phase of Mycenaean culture in Greece – the Shaft Grave Era – covers a period of about 150 years (*c.*1600–1450 BC) and is itself subdivided into two phases, one beginning early in the sixteenth century (LHI) and the other (LHIIA) lasting from around 1510 BC to 1450 BC.[1] Settlement evidence for the Shaft Grave Era is scarce, and much of what we learn about the Mycenaeans at this time comes from the burials of the dead. The tombs and those traces we do have of settlements show that the various areas of the mainland were progressing and developing at different rates; some far wealthier and more advanced than others. However, although the élite tomb types differed from region to region, their grave goods showed remarkable uniformity. Similar kinds of objects were used by people from different areas to express status and hierarchy, some of which have been found in tombs

27. Early Mycenaean gold goblet, c.1500 BC.

as far apart as the Argolid and Messenia. This shows that the ruling élites of these regional centres were in contact with each other and were either trading or exchanging prestigious items or employing the skills of travelling craftsmen.

These early Mycenaeans appear to have defined themselves and their status within the social hierarchy by certain types of artefacts, and it is by these same artefacts that we now define and identify the people we call 'Mycenaean'. Most common of these was pottery, accessible to all levels of society and found at all sites. The pottery in the sixteenth century BC (LHI) shows strong trends continuing from the Middle Bronze Age tradition, with large quantities of matt-painted and Minyan wares and comparatively small quantities of lustrous-painted early Mycenaean fine pottery. Artefacts belonging only to the élites of various areas include ornamental weapons and armour, fine jewellery, gold ornaments and vessels of precious metals. Although much of the gold in the burials was thin sheet gold, some items were certainly sturdy enough to have been used by their owners during their lifetime. Diadems placed in the tombs often show signs of wear, for instance. The fine jewellery would have been worn, too, and cups and jugs of gold and silver likewise must have once graced the feasting tables of these élites. The burial finds thus show that the upper echelons of society were very wealthy. However, when we look for suitable settings for such lives of relative wealth and sophistication, they are hard to find.

SETTLEMENTS

The picture that has emerged of the beginnings of Mycenaean culture is one of small but independent kingdoms – their boundaries often proscribed by natural geographical features – ruled by locally powerful chieftains. These regional chieftains appear to have lived in large buildings, the forerunners of the later palaces, but little remains of these structures. Although the people of the Shaft Grave Era had access to great wealth, they apparently did not invest it in their settlements. This is despite the fact that, as is clear from the construction of monumental tholos tombs, they had the expertise to build on a grand scale. It may simply be the accidents of excavation or the outcome of over-building, but it is not really until the second half of the fifteenth century (LHIIB), after the end of the Shaft Grave Era, that we start to get anything that looks remotely like a palace.

Where architectural remains have been identified and excavated, they are generally fairly simple and appear to have evolved out of the megaron house of the Middle Bronze Age, with a porch and a main room. More complex house forms, such as the sixteenth-century building at Peristeria, may perhaps be viewed as the forerunners of later mansions and palaces, with multiple rooms and a courtyard. There is little trace in the Shaft Grave Era of the architectural sophistication seen on contemporary Crete or on the mainland in later phases. Only at Mycenae and Tiryns, for example, have fresco fragments been found in levels attributable to the Shaft Grave Era, and on both sites these fragments appear to belong to the last phase of the period, in the first half of the fifteenth century. The paucity of fine architecture is echoed by the lack of fortification walls at most sites, though defensive walls, perhaps with watchtowers built into them, have been identified at Peristeria and at Pylos in Messenia – the latter incorporating a monumental gateway – and at the site of Kolonna on Aigina.

BURIALS

As we lack settlement sites, we have to rely heavily on the evidence from tombs for this period. The people of Mycenae itself were highly unusual in burying their chieftains and their families in shaft graves, though rare examples of the type have been found at Kolonna on Aegina and cut into the tumulus erected over the House of Tiles at Lerna. Some simple grave types persisted from the Middle Bronze Age, such as cist, pit and tumulus burials, but we also see the introduction of new tomb types, namely chamber tombs and stone-built tombs, the most complex of which was the tholos (round) or beehive tomb.

The chamber tomb was to become the standard form of Mycenaean burial, and large cemeteries of them have been found in all areas of the Mycenaean world. It was characterized by a long narrow entrance

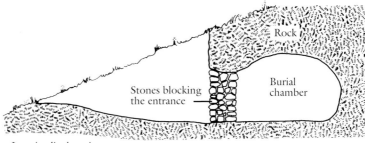

Rock

Burial chamber

Stones blocking the entrance

28. Plan of a chamber tomb.

Longitudinal section

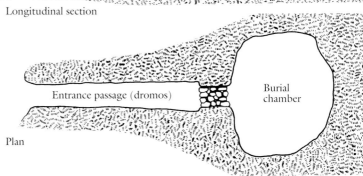

Entrance passage (dromos)

Burial chamber

Plan

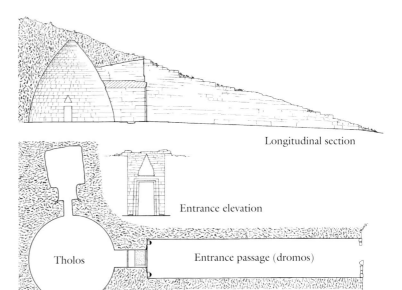

Longitudinal section

29. Plan of a tholos tomb.

Entrance elevation

Tholos

Entrance passage (dromos)

Plan

30. A chamber tomb at Mycenae, with the stone blocking of its doorway partially removed.

(dromos), a doorway (stomion) and a burial chamber cut out of the rock. Such tombs were usually cut into the hillside, but could be sunk into level ground and varied dramatically in size and complexity. The burial chamber itself was often irregular in shape and might have one or more side chambers leading off it. Multiple burials took place in these graves, with some tombs containing as many as twenty or more interments. Although mainly used for fairly simple burials, some very rich and splendid chamber tombs have been found: a large fourteenth-century example from the Kolonaki cemetery at Thebes had parallel double dromoi and fresco decoration, consisting of two figures of women painted on either side of the doorway; and a tomb at Argos also had its doorway decorated with frescoes, in this instance spirals.

Apart from at Mycenae, the preferred high-status grave of the Shaft Grave Era was the tholos or beehive tomb. Monumental and impressive, these stone-built tombs required a great deal of effort and

31. The Treasury of Atreus at Mycenae.

expertise to construct. The essential plan of the tholos was similar to that of the chamber tomb, with an entrance (dromos) leading to a doorway and thence to a large burial chamber. With the exception of one tomb at Thorikos, which had an oval-shaped burial chamber, the tholos was uniformly circular and had a corbelled roof. This tomb type showed a remarkable lack of diversity in shape and plan, though there was a traceable progression from early to later, more complex, examples. In this respect, the tholos was very different to the chamber tomb, which took a great variety of forms. Both were used for multiple burials, but there were comparatively fewer interments in the tholos.

The origins of the tholos are debated, with some taking the view that it evolved from the circular stone-built tombs of Minoan Crete, and others favouring a development from the Middle Bronze Age tumulus. The tholos tomb first made its appearance in Messenia and was adopted elsewhere on the mainland in the latter stages of the Shaft Grave Era, the early fifteenth century (LHIIA). A total of nine tholoi have been excavated at Mycenae and can be placed roughly chronologically into three groups of three according to their architectural sophistication: the Cyclopean Tomb, the Tomb of Aegisthus and Epano Phournos in the first group; the Lion Tomb, Panagia and Kato Phournos in the second group; and the Treasury of Atreus, Tomb of Clytemnestra and Tomb of the Genii in the third group. Six of the nine (the first two groups) were apparently all constructed in the first half of the fifteenth century. If this was indeed the case, then they cannot have been solely for royal burials, as six such tombs would surely not have been needed over a span of only fifty years. A unique form of stone-built tomb at Mycenae, belonging to this last phase of the Shaft Grave Era, is Tomb Rho, which was built into an earlier pre-existing tomb in Grave Circle B.

Tholos tombs were highly visible and had, for the most part, been very thoroughly robbed and ransacked by the time they were excavated; some appear to have been plundered not long after their last use. In the process, not only are rich finds removed but the tomb is disturbed, with important evidence being destroyed that would allow us to interpret the death rituals that took place at the time of burial. Robbers gaining access to the tomb would find the dead lying on the floor of the chamber, though in some burials the body was placed in a pit or cist dug into the floor and therefore escaped the notice of the tomb's despoilers.

Where we do find undisturbed burials in tholos and chamber tombs, we discover that they were similar in form to those of the shaft graves at Mycenae: almost uniformly inhumations rather than cremations and accompanied by grave goods appropriate to sex and status. Signs of funerary feasting and animal sacrifice have been found at some tombs: smashed *kylikes* (stemmed goblets) in the dromos indicating ritual drinking, and the bones of sacrificial sheep and goats suggesting a funerary meal at the grave. Sacrificed dogs were probably placed in the tomb to act as its guardian or to accompany the dead in the afterlife, and horses (sometimes in pairs) in the dromos may be those that pulled the chariot or funerary cart carrying the dead to the tomb. After the initial burial, the doorway of the tomb was blocked with stones. When it was re-used for the next burial, some of the stones were removed and the tomb was fumigated with clay braziers, which are often found *in situ*. Earlier burials in the chamber sometimes had to be moved aside to make room for the latest interment. The tomb was then closed again by re-blocking the doorway with stones.

32. Clay braziers were placed in the tomb to fumigate it for subsequent burials.

RELIGION

The limitations of having to rely so heavily on tomb evidence for this period are evident when we try to examine religious belief and ritual, other than those associated with funerary practices. It is difficult, for instance, in these early years to distinguish Mycenaean religious behaviour and belief from that of the Minoans, given the number of Minoan imports and iconographical influences seen on the mainland. It is unclear to what extent, if any, religious beliefs were imported with the religious iconography. At only one place on the mainland, the site of the later sanctuary to Apollo Maleatas near Epidauros, do we have what may be a shrine or identifiable cult place datable to the Shaft Grave Era; bronze double-axes, a fragment of a steatite *rhyton* (decorated with figures in relief) and seals associated with animal bones and burnt material have been found there.

THE REGIONS

The Argolid

It seems from the evidence of tombs that Mycenae held a position of unchallenged pre-eminence in the north-east Peloponnese. The grave circles and nine tholos tombs are part of a great cemetery on the south-west slopes of Mycenae, and the number of early graves excavated has revealed that there was a sizeable population living there in the Shaft Grave Era. A search for the living quarters of those buried at Mycenae has yielded little. From the beginnings of the Shaft Grave Era blocks of limestone still bearing traces of red stucco have been found below the later palace, and from near the end of the period come scraps of fresco decoration. This seems to indicate some level of sophisticated building at the site, but if there were fine buildings on the acropolis of Mycenae then subsequent rebuilding and expansion have all but obliterated them.

Despite the undoubted pre-eminence of Mycenae, there were other flourishing centres in the Argolid. Tiryns, so important in later centuries, has only a few architectural remains belonging to the Shaft Grave Era, but they are enough to show that the settlement was quite substantial at the time. As at Mycenae, fresco fragments have been found on the acropolis. Here, too, was unearthed a rich treasure, probably from an ancient tomb-robbers hoard. If it did indeed come from an early tholos tomb at Tiryns, as has been suggested, it would indicate that the site had access to at least some of the wealth of nearby Mycenae. An extensive cemetery of chamber tombs on the nearby Prophitis Ilias hill shows that the settlement was sizeable.

Elsewhere in the Argolid it is hard to draw too many conclusions about the number and size of settlements, which are often only indicated by the cemeteries that held their dead. Tholos tombs dating to the first half of the fifteenth century, indicating the presence of important centres nearby, have been discovered at Berbati close to Mycenae, at Prosymna (which also has a cemetery of chamber tombs containing some rich burials), and at Kokla (where an unrobbed tholos tomb and a cemetery of chamber tombs have been found). The Kokla tholos, some 5 km (3 miles) from Argos, dates to the early fifteenth century and had a façade decorated with frescoes. It contained rich grave goods – including a drinking set of silver conical cups and *kylikes* – but no human remains, indicating that it may have been a cenotaph, perhaps erected in honour of a death at sea or in foreign lands. The north-east Peloponnese was clearly home to thriving élites in the Shaft Grave Era, not only at Mycenae and Tiryns, but also at smaller sites scattered in the Argive plain.

Messenia

At the opposite corner of the Peloponnese, to the south-west in the area now known as Messenia, it is evident that the early Mycenaeans were also establishing a number of settlements. There had been little sign of prosperity in Messenia until fairly late in the Middle Bronze Age, but by the time of the Shaft Grave Era a number of wealthy centres ruled by local chieftains had emerged in the region. The many early tholoi in the area are our best clue as to the whereabouts and number of these local centres and it seems the tholos tomb was first adopted in the region. On the coast, at Voidhokoilia on the Koryphasion peninsula, is a very early example, dug into an existing Middle Bronze Age tumulus. Known as the Tomb of Thrasymedes, it is apparently the earliest tholos in Messenia and quite possibly in the entire mainland.

In later years Messenia was to be dominated by the great Mycenaean palace at Pylos, built on the hill of Epano Englianos and named by its excavator the 'Palace of Nestor', after the legendary king made famous in epic poetry. However, the coastal plain around the Navarino Bay, which later was to provide the milieu in which the Palace of Nestor developed, was home to several centres associated with tholos tombs in the Shaft Grave Era. The site of the future palace was already a significant centre; traces of a fortification wall show that the low hill was defended and a massive gateway gave access on the north-west side. The nearby burials are further testimony to the settlement's importance. Two of the four Pylos tholos tombs belong to the Shaft Grave Era – Tomb IV dating from the sixteenth century (LHI) and Tomb II the first half of the fifteenth century (LHIIA) – as do the 'Grave Circle' (a multiple tomb which may have been roofed) and chamber tombs. When it was excavated, it was found that Tomb IV still contained remnants of its rich grave goods, including a fine large gold seal decorated with a crowned griffin with outstretched wings. This was, perhaps, the royal seal of the rulers of Pylos as the throne of the later palace was flanked by a pair of griffins painted on the wall behind it.

The site of Peristeria in Messenia rivalled and perhaps even outshone Pylos in the Shaft Grave Era, with a fortification wall and a large building dating back to the sixteenth century. Three tholos tombs associated with the settlement date to the Shaft Grave Era and further demonstrate the importance of the site at the time. The smallest and earliest of these, Tomb 3 (dated to the sixteenth century) contained a body laid on the floor, with clay vases and rich grave goods in a shallow pit in the ground. The riches buried there comprised a gold diadem decorated with bosses, small gold cut-out ornaments for attachment to clothing, gold tassels, three gold cups and fragments of bronze inlaid with a fleur-de-lis, a leaf and a dolphin's head. These objects clearly belong to the same milieu as those from the shaft graves at Mycenae, and some of them may even have been made by the same craftsmen. The other two tholoi had been robbed, but scattered fragments of gold and stone vessels, jewellery and fine vases indicate that they once contained very rich burials. The nature of these burials, both the high-status tomb types and the character of the grave goods, shows that Peristeria was rich and powerful in the Shaft Grave Era.

Many other parts of Messenia apparently had settlements ruled by local chieftains. At Nichoria tholos tombs have been found associated with a large building of the fifteenth century and rich tombs at Kakovatos and Routsi-Myrsinochorion point to the existence of important settlements in the Shaft Grave Era, even if little or no trace of them has yet been found. At Routsi-Myrsinochorion an unrobbed tholos tomb was discovered with the final burial in the tomb preserved intact. On the floor of the tomb lay a warrior burial of a man, who had been placed on a red-and-blue rush mat or blanket. He wore a necklace of amber beads and was accompanied by ten swords and daggers, as well as by personal items such as a mirror and a number of gems and seals. Earlier burials were also found in the tomb, placed in two cist graves dug into the chamber floor, their contents dating to the Shaft Grave Era, with vases dating mostly to the first half of the fifteenth century (LHIIA). One contained a burial of a woman wearing a necklace; and the other four or five burials were accompanied by grave goods that included two particularly beautiful inlaid daggers of the kind found in the shaft graves at Mycenae, one decorated with stalking leopards and the other with swimming argonauts. On the floor of the chamber, between the two cist graves, was a clay tripod brazier decorated with an octopus, presumably for fumigating the tomb when it was reopened for subsequent burials.

Messenia was thus demonstrably home to a lively and vibrant culture in the Shaft Grave Era, with close ties to that of the Argive plain. Other regions of the Peloponnese clearly had flourishing local centres, but none of them rivalled Messenia and the Argolid in their number.

Laconia

Laconia, for instance, only shows patches of prosperity at this time. The tholos tomb at Vapheio, dating to the end of the Shaft Grave Era, though robbed and ruined nevertheless preserved a chieftain burial of the first half of the fifteenth century (LHIIA) in a pit in the chamber floor. Richly adorned with jewellery (seals at his wrists, rings, necklaces of Baltic amber and a double string of amethyst beads), this warrior lay accompanied by personal items, such as a mirror, and by many weapons, including a long sword, two large spears, nine daggers and knives, a pair of axes, a gold-plated dagger and a dagger inlaid with a scene of men swimming. At each hand lay two cups of precious metal, one of gold and one of silver. The pair of gold Vapheio cups (fig. 33) have given their name to all cups of the same shape, and were decorated in *repoussé* with scenes of bull-hunting and capture – one a peaceful scene and the other far more violent. It has been plausibly suggested that the former is of Minoan manufacture, whereas the latter is Mycenaean.[2] The range of goods from the Vapheio tholos includes beads of amber from the Baltic, imports from Minoan Crete and a ring of iron – a rare and precious metal at the time – thus demonstrating that by the latter stages of the Shaft Grave Era the ruling élite of Mycenaean Laconia had access to the same wealth and trading links as the chieftains of the Argolid and Messenia.

The chieftain buried in the Vapheio tholos probably ruled the nearby settlement of Palaiopyrgi, which must therefore have been an important local centre in the Shaft Grave Era, as were the Menelaion (on a low hill close to the town of modern Sparta) and Ayios Stephanos

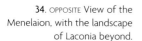

33. Pair of gold cups from a tholos tomb at Vapheio, decorated with scenes of bull capture.

34. OPPOSITE View of the Menelaion, with the landscape of Laconia beyond.

(on the coast). The latter perhaps derived its wealth from the export of *Lapis lacedaimonios*, a fine Laconian stone prized by the Minoans.

Elsewhere in the Peloponnese there is not much evidence of great prosperity in the Shaft Grave Era. Arcadia, for instance, has produced few significant remains for this period, save for some tombs at Analipsis; and the Korinthia, adjacent to the Argolid in the north-east Peloponnese, as yet has shown little sign of its neighbour's wealth.

North of the Peloponnese we do find other flourishing centres of early Mycenaean culture. In Attica local settlements appear to have been focused at Athens, Thorikos and Marathon – with some traces at Brauron and Eleusis – and at Kolonna on the island of Aigina. Further north again, in the area of central Greece, a cemetery of chamber tombs with some rich burials of the first half of the fifteenth century (LHIIA) have been found near Thebes in Boiotia, the site of a later Mycenaean palace. The lack of settlement material from Thebes in the Shaft Grave Era may be a result of the difficulties of excavating the site, which is built over by the modem town. In Thessaly the only site of any importance was Volos (ancient Iolkos), which gave access from the coast to the inland areas – a strategic position for trade and the source of its prosperity. The Kapakli tholos, excavated in the region of Volos, had collapsed and therefore escaped being robbed. It contained some gold jewellery and scraps of ivory, but the contents were very poor and limited when compared with those from other tholoi elsewhere in the contemporary Mycenaean world.

TRADE IN THE SHAFT GRAVE ERA

The similarities between these developing regional centres of six-teenth- and early fifteenth-century BC mainland Greece (LHI–IIA) are a testimony to the strong internal trading routes that must have linked them to each other. The establishment of a ruling élite at many places on the mainland, demonstrating its power and authority by means of conspicuous displays of wealth, was a huge boost to trade. The Myce-naeans had the resources to import luxuries, a wide range of raw materials not available to them in their own land and, apparently, the services of skilled craftsmen from abroad. Although some of the finds from the Shaft Grave Era were surely made by Mycenaean craftsmen, others used sophisticated techniques already employed by the Minoans. Moreover, certain kinds of objects, such as the inlaid daggers, were probably made especially for the Mycenaeans by Minoan crafts-men.

The extraordinary wealth which characterizes the Shaft Grave Era sets apart the early Mycenaeans from their Middle Bronze Age prede-cessors, who lived in relative poverty and mostly relied on local resources. Where did this sudden wealth come from? Scientific analy-sis of metals has suggested that the Mycenaeans acquired this prosper-ity by exploiting sources of copper, silver and lead at mines at Laurion in Attica – already mined for silver in the Early Bronze Age – thus becoming key players in the metals trade in the Mediterranean. Cop-per, essential to a culture dependent on bronze, was for a long time thought to have been imported into the Mycenaean world, with Cyprus as the main source. More recently, however, scientific analysis has indicated that much Mycenaean copper was mined locally at Lau-rion. Furthermore, a study of ingots found on Crete has shown that the Minoans, too, were importing copper from Laurion by the early fif-teenth century, as well as, to a lesser extent, from Cyprus and Sardinia (their principal sources had been Syria and Mesopotamia in the early sixteenth century). Silver from the shaft graves at Mycenae has also been analyzed and much of it is from Laurion, although some is clearly imported from elsewhere.

The mining of copper, silver and lead at Laurion would not only have satisfied the Mycenaeans' own needs but could have provided them with a surplus of valuable goods for trading purposes. Their pre-cious metals at home could be exchanged for those from abroad, notably tin and gold. Quantities of tin would have to be imported to alloy with copper to make bronze, and the Mycenaeans probably traded their silver for tin, which, whatever its ultimate source, seems likely to have been imported from the East. The sheer amount of gold buried in the graves of the Shaft Grave Era shows a great demand for it. It is unlikely that the Mycenaeans were already exploiting those Aegean sources of gold known from the later historical period –

namely the islands of Siphnos and Thasos – so the metal probably came from Egypt.

When we look out from the Aegean to the wider world of Mediterranean trade, it appears that the Mycenaeans were tapping into these trade routes via the Minoans on Crete. Supplying the Minoans with metals from Laurion could have given the Mycenaeans access, in exchange, to goods available on existing trade routes from Egypt and the Near East.

By the early sixteenth century, at the start of the Shaft Grave Era, the Minoans had already established a network of trading routes encompassing the Aegean islands and had founded colonies on several of them – at Kastri on Kythera, Serraglio on Kos, Trianda on Rhodes, and perhaps Akrotiri on Thera. Abroad, the Minoans were again demonstrably the main force in the Aegean, trading widely with the Near East and with Egypt. The Minoans seem also to have established colonies on the coast of Asia Minor, at Iasos and Miletos, using them to further their trading interests in the area.

Contacts between the Minoans and Egypt appear to have been established as early as the Early Bronze Age (Early Minoan II), with

35. *Alabastron* decorated with argonauts and seaweed and *rhyton* (ritual sprinkling vessel) decorated with stylized plants. Both were found in Egypt and date to 1500–1450 BC.

some raw materials probably coming from Egypt – gold, amethyst and carnelian, for example, as well as perhaps hippopotamus ivory. By the Shaft Grave Era, links between the Minoans and Egypt had intensified and Egyptian iconographical motifs were adopted by the Minoans, such as Ta-urt (Taweret) – the Egyptian hippopotamus goddess – who became a fertility genius of Minoan and then Mycenaean iconography. Over in Egypt, Minoan pottery has been found at Twelfth Dynasty (nineteenth century BC) levels of sites such as Kahun, Abydos, Harageh, el-Lisht and Qubet el Hawa. From early Thirteenth Dynasty (in the first half of the eighteenth century BC) contexts at Tell el Dab'a come fragments of Minoan Kamares Ware pottery cups and, from the same site, jewellery from a robbed tomb, including an Aegean-looking gold pendant of antithetical dogs. The discovery here, too, of Minoan frescoes depicting bull-leaping in palatial buildings of the Late Hyksos/early Eighteenth Dynasty (c.1540 BC) have revealed hitherto unsuspected levels of contact, the significance of which is still hotly debated. Minoan-style frescoes have also been found in the Near East, at Tel Atchana, Tell el Kabri, and possibly also at Qatna.

New Kingdom contacts between the Minoans and Egyptians are graphically attested on wall paintings in Egyptian tombs. Actual Minoans are only painted on the walls of six tombs – those of Senmut, Puyemre, Intef, Useramun, Menkheperreseneb and Rekhmire (fig. 38) – spanning the reigns of Hatshepsut, Thutmose III and the beginning of that of Amenhotep II. The last depiction of true Minoans in tomb paintings therefore dates to shortly after 1450 BC.

The Minoans were thus busy both in the Aegean and further afield, and their activities brought benefits in turn to the Mycenaeans. The tombs of the Shaft Grave Era on the mainland, especially those from Mycenae itself, demonstrate that the Mycenaeans were indeed exploiting their own sources of wealth to gain access to the trade goods acquired by the Minoans. A strong Minoan influence, clearly intensifying throughout the Shaft Grave Era, is evident in the grave goods of the early Mycenaeans. The faience – in the form of sacral knots and vessels – found in the Mycenae shaft graves, for example, belongs to a well-established Minoan tradition. In fact, many of the items in the graves once thought to have an Egyptian provenance are far more likely to have reached the Mycenaeans indirectly via Crete. Ostrich eggs used to make the *rhyta* (ritual sprinkling vessels) found in Graves IV and V of Circle A at Mycenae probably came from Nubia, via the port of Marsa Matruh on the Egyptian coast. They appear, though, to have first reached Crete, where craftsmen added faience fittings and dolphin appliqués of purely Minoan style. Semi-precious stones from abroad also probably came via Crete, with amethyst, for instance, being imported from Egypt. However, a local amethyst from the Peloponnese may perhaps have been used for a necklace found in Grave IV at Mycenae.

Whole classes of objects appear not to be imports as such, but rather to have been made by Cretan artists and craftsmen catering for specifically Mycenaean tastes. This would explain the phenomenon of what looks like Minoan workmanship applied to apparently Mycenaean types of object. Typical of such products are the inlaid daggers, found only in the Peloponnese save for one lone example from the island of Thera. It is clear also that mainland craftsmen were influenced by Minoan styles and techniques, producing imitations and adaptations of Minoan pottery shapes and decorative motifs for the Mycenaean market.

Some types of object, though, do not perhaps fit this pattern of trade and exchange. Baltic amber, for instance, used to make the necklaces so popular with Mycenaean warriors, must have travelled over long land trade routes to reach the Greek mainland from the Baltic Sea. This trade can be traced in the archaeological record. Intriguingly, a particular form of amber spacing bead appears in a few items of jewellery (for example, an amber necklace from Grave Omicron in Circle B at Mycenae), dating to a short time-span early in the sixteenth century. This type of bead has its closest parallels in the Upton Lovell necklace from the contemporary Bronze Age Wessex Culture in Britain, and some have suggested this might indicate an isolated example of direct trade between the two cultures.

Other items found in high-status graves may have reached the Shaft Grave Era Mycenaeans not through trade but rather as highly prized items of gift-exchange between ruling élites from different regions. The rock-crystal duck bowl (fig. 13) from Grave Omicron in Grave Circle B, for instance, carved as it was out of a single piece of crystal, must have been an object of extreme rarity and value. Despite the Egyptianizing style of this bowl, it belongs firmly to the tradition of Minoan stone-vessel carving and may have been a present from the Minoans on Crete to the newly wealthy rulers on the mainland. Similarly, the silver stag *rhyton* from Grave IV in Circle A is a rare example of an import from the Hittite Empire of Anatolia. This may perhaps also have been a gift, given at a time when the two great Bronze Age warrior cultures of the Mycenaeans and Hittites had yet to fall out with each other over conflicting interests in Asia Minor.

Although it is evident that the Minoans were dominating trade in the Aegean and beyond in the Shaft Grave Era, the Mycenaeans were also consolidating relationships and pushing boundaries. For instance, the links between them and the Cycladic islands, already established in the Middle Bronze Age, were strengthened in this period. Small quantities of Mycenaean pottery from the sixteenth century (LHI) have also been found further afield, for example to the west on the Aeolian island of Lipari and the island of Vivara opposite Naples, and to the east at Miletos on the coast of Asia Minor. Later in the Shaft Grave Era, in the first half of the fifteenth century (LHIIA), Mycenaean pottery also reached such sites as Troy and Kazanli in Asia Minor, Ayia lrini on the island of Cyprus, Lachish and Tell Ajjul in Palestine, Byblos in the Lebanon and Saqqara and Gurob in Egypt.

During the Shaft Grave Era we are almost entirely dependent on the evidence of pottery when we try to look for signs of the Mycenaeans outside the confines of the mainland. Moreover, we have to bear in mind that these pots may well have been traded on by others. However, from the island of Thera – one of the Cycladic islands some 62 km (38 miles) north of Crete – comes a vivid depiction of the Mycenaeans abroad. Thera had suffered a violent volcanic eruption around

36. Marching Mycenaean warriors on a miniature wall painting from Akrotiri on Thera.

1540 BC, which blew the heart out of the island and showered what remained of it with volcanic ash and pumice. Digging down through this volcanic debris, excavators discovered a town in an extraordinarily fine state of preservation, likened by some to a Bronze Age Pompeii.

With its streets, squares, houses and shrines, the town of Akrotiri vividly brings to life the scanty remains we have from other Late Bronze Age settlements of the sixteenth century. The walls of some of the buildings were decorated with brightly coloured wall paintings, which included depictions of the people of the town. Although the majority of the human figures painted on the Thera frescoes are no doubt the Therans themselves, other types of people are represented and amongst them we find the Mycenaeans. On a miniature frieze from the north wall of the West House at Thera we see a scene of ships arriving at a coastal settlement (presumably on Thera itself), where men are drowning in the water and a row of warriors are marching inland (figs 36 and 61). The warriors are identified as Mycenaeans by their boar's-tusk helmets and large rectangular ox-hide shields. They carry long spears and have tasselled swords slung at their waists.[3] Further up the hill the local people are going about their ordinary daily tasks: women are drawing water from a well and men are leading their flocks to pasture. At the top of the hill a ceremony of some kind is taking place.

CONCLUSION

When we look at the picture on the Greek mainland in the Middle Bronze Age and compare it with the splendid ostentation and vigour of the early Mycenaeans in the Shaft Grave Era, it is clear that life had improved exponentially in a very short period of time. These changes at home, however, were as yet not reflected in the balance of power in the Aegean. Crete remained dominant in the region: flourishing at home, establishing colonies on some of the islands and exerting a strong influence on others. But the warlike nature of the Mycenaeans must have made them a force to be reckoned with in the Aegean, as the Thera fresco so dramatically demonstrates, and by the end of the Shaft Grave Era major changes were afoot.

5

Minoans, Mycenaeans and the Winds of Change

By the middle of the fifteenth century BC the last burial had been made in the shaft graves of Mycenae, rich tholos tombs lay scattered across many areas of the mainland, Mycenaean pottery was reaching sites as far away as Gurob in Egypt and Troy in Anatolia, and the winds of change were beginning to blow across the Aegean.

DESTRUCTIONS ON CRETE c.1450 BC

As the Shaft Grave Era drew to a close the people of Crete suffered a violent reversal of fortune. Around 1450 BC the palaces, villas and towns of the Minoans, hitherto secure and predominant in the Aegean, were hit by a great wave of destructions. All the major sites, with the exception of Knossos, succumbed: Mallia on the north coast, Phaistos inland to the south, Zakros far flung to the east and Khania to the west were wiped out as palace centres. The destructions affected Knossos town and some of the surrounding buildings, but the palace itself was spared. Henceforth the numbers of Minoan imports to areas previously receiving them declined dramatically and in Egypt – from shortly after 1450 BC – true Minoans were no longer portrayed on tomb paintings. Tombs subsequently purporting to portray Keftiu (the Egyptian name for the Minoans) – those of Amenemhab, Kenemun and Anen – show either hybrid figures or ones that have little in common with earlier depictions. This calamity that had befallen the Minoans was to have momentous consequences for the Mycenaeans.

Arthur Evans, excavating at Knossos, recognized that pottery from the palace was later in date than that found in destruction layers at other sites on the island. He also felt that Knossos in its final phase, having outlived the other palatial centres, had a more militaristic and bureaucratic air than in earlier times. He therefore argued that Knossos had turned on and destroyed the other palaces on the island, establishing a powerful dynasty that held sway on Crete until Knossos, too, fell in its turn, prey to a great earthquake and to fire.

A different explanation for the downfall of the Minoans was put forward by the Greek archaeologist Spiridon Marinatos, who was excavating the Minoan villa site of Amnisos on the north coast of Crete in the 1930s and found there several blocks of a wall overturned. He envisaged a great tidal wave devastating Crete, caused by a violent volcanic eruption on the island of Thera to the north.[1] This theory, whilst an attractive one, will no longer bear close scrutiny. It is hard to see, for instance, how a tidal wave could have brought down the palace of Phaistos, inland and sited on a high ridge in the south of the island, and how it could have selectively damaged buildings in the environs of Knossos but spared the palace itself. Likewise, if there really had been widespread and catastrophic devastation of the Cretan countryside by such a phenomenon, it is hard to understand the prosperity of the final phase of the palace at Knossos.

Once excavations at the site of Akrotiri on Thera were under way, other problems with Marinatos' theory became apparent. Found in the ruins were quantities of datable Minoan pottery. The destruction level on Crete contained pottery of Late Minoan Ib style (dating to about 1450 BC), whereas that from Akrotiri was of Late Minoan Ia style (about 1540 BC) – a gap of some ninety years between the two events. It appears that the Therans had warning of imminent disaster and had fled Akrotiri before the final eruption enveloped their town. Is it then possible that the Therans fled in 1540 BC, leaving behind them pottery of LMIa style, and that the eruption of the volcano occurred some ninety years later, causing the destructions on Crete?[2]

It is clear from the excavations that before the site was abandoned, Akrotiri had been shaken by small earth tremors: fragile pots, for instance, have been found placed in safe areas within the houses. It then seems that the people left the site, taking with them their valuables as none have been found in the ruins. The deserted town was then hit by more severe earthquakes, causing considerable damage to its buildings. The angry rumblings must then have ceased for a time, as some of the people returned to their town and made attempts to repair their homes. Final warning of impending disaster caused the Therans once again to flee, and they seem to have made their escape before the town of Akrotiri was buried by the erupting volcano as no bodies have been discovered in the ruins. The consensus of opinion amongst volcanologists is that the span of time between the earthquakes shaking the island and the eruption, or several eruptions, of the volcano could be no more than three years, far from the ninety years needed to equate the eruption with the destructions on Crete.[3]

The traditional date for the eruption of Thera derived from the archaeological evidence is around 1540 BC. Scientists studying data from tree-rings and ice-cores have dated the eruption some hundred years earlier, but corroboration of the later date has now come from the site of Tell el Dab'a in Egypt: pumice found at the site, in contexts dating to around 1540 BC, has been proven scientifically to come from Thera. Even disregarding the absolute chronology of the phases of Late Minoan la and lb, the argument based on the relative chronology still

37. Excavation at the Late
Bronze Age town of Akrotiri
on Thera.

holds; the pottery found at Akrotiri belongs to a phase earlier than that in the destructions on Crete.

If the eruption of Thera did not destroy the Minoan civilization on Crete, then what did? Toppled walls, such as those previously noted at Amnisos, have led some to believe the cause was a great earthquake similar to that which destroyed the Old Palaces on Crete around 1700 BC. An earthquake, like a tsunami, though, would not have discriminated between the houses at Knossos and the palace. Furthermore, after the 1700 BC earthquake the Minoans rebuilt and went on to grow in prosperity; the aftermath of the 1450 BC disaster was very different.

A.J.B. Wace, excavating at Mycenae, took up the militaristic arguments put forward by Evans, but gave them a decidedly different slant. In his eyes the differences between the final phase at Knossos and those that preceded it were so great as to indicate an entirely different people in control of the palace. He argued that it was the warlike Mycenaeans of the mainland who had taken over Crete and established themselves at Knossos. There were things about Knossos in its final phase that appeared to be more Mycenaean than Minoan – such as certain pottery types, architectural features and elements of the fresco paintings – though all of these could be explained in ways other than a Mycenaean take-over. More interesting was the appearance of warrior burials on Crete after the destructions of 1450 BC, of a type so familiar from the cemeteries of the Mycenaeans, and the sporadic building of tholos tombs of mainland type.

The most telling argument in favour of a Mycenaean take-over of Knossos is that several thousand tablets inscribed with Linear B were found in the ruins of the palace, baked hard in the final conflagration. Thus Linear B, the script of the Mycenaeans, and not Linear A, the script of the Minoans, was used by the rulers of Knossos in its last years. Furthermore, the tablets reveal that the rulers of Knossos exercised wide-ranging control over much of the island. If one looks back at the mainland for evidence that the Mycenaeans were indeed in control of Crete from 1450 BC, there is no sign of intensifying links with the island until the early fourteenth century. From the tomb paintings of Egypt, however, comes a small and intriguing piece of evidence: in the tomb of Rekhmire, portrayals of Keftiu have had the usual form of Minoan kilt painted over and replaced by a new one which looks much more Mycenaean, perhaps reflecting Egyptian recognition of a change of dress at Knossos (fig. 38). Was this brought about by the presence there of Mycenaean rulers?[4]

MYCENAEANS TAKE CONTROL

The destructions of c.1450 BC on Crete had a dramatic effect on the Aegean. The Minoans' reversal of fortune at home was naturally enough reflected in their position abroad, and imports of Minoan pottery to the mainland and the islands declined dramatically. The Mycenaeans, however, did not immediately fill the vacuum left by the demise of the Minoans. Mycenaean pottery dating to the latter half of the fifteenth century (LHIIB) did reach the Aegean islands and further afield to places like Cyprus, Amman in the Near East, Lahun in Egypt, Apulia and the Lipari Islands and Troy, but the quantities were relatively small. In the early fourteenth century, though, the Mycenaeans began fully to take advantage of the opportunities presented by the misfortunes of the Minoans. This phase (LHIIIA1) was clearly a key one for the Mycenaeans. On the Greek mainland large proto-palatial structures were built at sites like Tiryns, Thebes, Nichoria, Pylos, Volos and the Menelaion at Sparta – for the first time giving us the homes of the Mycenaean ruling élite. The people were also building houses of varying size, such as the large Ramp House at Mycenae, probably reflecting the differing wealth and status of those who lived in them. A hoard of treasure found by Schliemann on the acropolis of Mycenae, dating to the mid-fifteenth to mid-fourteenth centuries (LHIIB–IIIA1), included fine gold goblets with dog-head handles, a large plain gold cup and gold and silver jewellery and testifies to the richness of the rulers of Mycenae at this time.

The Mycenaeans also began to expand outside the mainland, establishing settlements on some of the islands. Rhodes, a useful stop-over point on trade routes to the East, attracted Mycenaean settlers in the years after the Minoan destructions. Mycenaean pottery of the second half of the fifteenth century (LHIIB) has been found at the Minoan colony of Trianda on the coast, which was abandoned in the early years of the fourteenth century; the Mycenaeans appear to have established their own settlement nearby, a little further inland, at Ialysos. Cemeteries of Mycenaean tombs, dating from the second half of the fifteenth century through to the twelfth, contained the customary weapons, jewellery, ivory carving, and fine- and coarse-ware pottery that were characteristic of a flourishing Mycenaean community, though their settlement has yet to be found. Such communities clearly retained close ties with the mainland, even importing much of their fine pottery from the Argolid rather than making it locally. On the nearby island of Kos a Mycenaean settlement has been excavated at Serraglio, and settlements of similar status at Langanda and Eleona are indicated by chamber-tomb cemeteries found there.

The prosperity of the Mycenaeans at home is also seen abroad as they began to expand into trade routes established by the Minoans. The Mycenaeans were exporting their pottery to Crete and sites on the Aegean islands such as Phylakopi on Melos and Ayia Irini on Kea. Further afield, Mycenaean pottery was reaching Enkomi, Hala Sultan Tekké, Maroni and Kalavassos on Cyprus, and sites on the coast of Asia Minor such as Troy and Miletos. In the Near East, Mycenaean pottery was reaching many places, notably Tell el Sa'idiyeh, Gezer, El Jib, Hazor and Tell Kazel, and to the west trade continued with the Aeolian Islands and as far away as Llanetede Los Moros in Spain.

There have been suggestions of direct links between the Mycenaeans and Egyptians at this time, even to the extent of the pharaoh Amenhotep III (1390–1352 BC) sending a formal diplomatic mission to the Aegean: objects bearing the cartouche of Amenhotep III and his wife Queen Tiye have been found at Mycenae and Tiryns. In addition, a statue base at Kom el Hetan in Egypt was inscribed with a list of place-names in the Aegean, including Knossos and Mycenae, possibly recording the itinerary of such a mission.

Thus the Mycenaeans, after an apparent initial hesitation, had begun to move into the position of pre-eminence in the Aegean once held by the Minoans. Around the middle of the fourteenth century, though, there are signs of some disruption and localized destructions on mainland sites like Mycenae, Tiryns and Athens, and important buildings at Nichoria in Messenia and the Menelaion at Sparta suffered serious damage and were subsequently abandoned. A further sign of dislocation was that some tholos tombs, used for multiple burials over several generations, appear to have gone out of use in this period.

38. Wall painting from the tomb of Rekhmire, Egypt, showing Aegeans bringing offerings to the pharaoh.

THE FALL OF KNOSSOS

These pockets of difficulty on the mainland – often of unknown cause – were reflected on a larger scale on Crete, where Knossos appears to have met its final end as a palace. The date of this event has provoked intense debate and controversy, at the heart of which are the three thousand or so clay tablets inscribed with Linear B script, found when the site was excavated. The destruction has traditionally been dated on archaeological grounds to around 1375 BC, at which time Knossos was believed to have stopped functioning as a palatial centre. Traces of subsequent occupation on a much smaller scale in the thirteenth century suggest that survivors were eking out a living in the ruins. That this reoccupation was by Minoans and not by an intrusive people is indicated by the style and manufacture of their pottery and in their observances of cult, seen for instance at the Shrine of the Double Axes. In the second half of the thirteenth century even this limited life at the site was to end, with a sudden and apparently complete abandonment, which was echoed elsewhere on Crete at town sites such as Gournia and Palaikastro.

This then is the picture traditionally presented of the fate of final-phase Knossos. It has, however, been strenuously and vehemently challenged. In the 1960s a philologist, Leonard Palmer, argued that the end of the palace at Knossos had come not in 1375 but considerably

later, roughly at the same time as the wave of destructions that hit the mainland palaces at the end of the thirteenth century. His theory depended on an examination of the Linear B tablets found in the ruins, which exhibited the same scripts, spellings, dialects and scribal conventions as those from Pylos. He suggested it was unlikely that two such similar bodies of tablets could have been separated by 175 years and argued that those from Knossos must also belong to the thirteenth century, showing that the site was still a flourishing palace centre at that time. A spirited defence of the 1375 BC date was made on archaeological grounds (led in print by John Boardman), based for instance on evidence that the tablets were found in levels below those of the thirteenth-century reoccupation.[5] This was supported on philological grounds by scholars like John Chadwick.

Several arguments to support Palmer's hypothesis have since been put forward. Khania on Crete has been identified as the source of many of the stirrup-jars inscribed in Linear B with personal and place-names known from the Knossos tablets that have been found at mainland sites like Mycenae, Tiryns, Orchomenos and Thebes. In 1962 such inscribed jars were found also at Khania, the first discovery of Linear B on Crete outside Knossos. They date to the thirteenth century, isolating Knossos still further in its early date for Linear B. Some scholars working on the handwriting of scribes believe they have discovered the same scribe at work both at Khania and at Knossos, a further indication, if true, that they were indeed contemporaneous. Amid all this evidence the debate rages as fiercely as ever.

Back on the mainland the Mycenaeans entered a period of stability, which was to stretch into the latter years of the thirteenth century and was reflected at home in monumental building, flourishing settlements and rich cemeteries. The Mycenaeans were now dominant in the Aegean, and thus began the era of the Mycenaean 'koine' – a highly uniform culture that spread across mainland Greece and the islands.

39. OPPOSITE Large *krater* (bowl) from Ialysos, Rhodes, of the fourteenth century BC, decorated with an octopus.

6

Palaces and Kingdoms of the Mycenaeans

As the power and influence of the Mycenaeans grew in the Aegean during the fourteenth and thirteenth centuries BC, they transformed the land in which they lived, building great and sumptuous palaces at the heart of their kingdoms, often protected by imposing fortification walls of massive Cyclopean masonry.[1] Henceforth, the wealth deposited in tombs in earlier years was to be found lavished on the homes of the ruling élite. The Mycenaean palaces, though, were not simply the home of the king, his family and his court, but, as Minoan palaces before them, combined many functions: residential, state and ceremonial rooms co-existed with areas set aside for observances of religious ritual, for workshops and for storage.

The building of these palace kingdoms marked a distinct shift in settlement patterns from that established during the Shaft Grave Era. The various regions of Mycenaean Greece were no longer home to a number of apparently independent chiefdoms; centralized states of great social and political sophistication and complexity were established in their place. Sites in Messenia, for instance, which were formerly independent – like Nichoria (which rivalled Pylos in importance in the Shaft Grave Era) – now seemed to be under the direct control of the palace at Pylos (if its correlation with the place named *ti-mi-to-a-ke-e* in Linear B is correct, as seems likely). Those who lived in the palaces clearly exercised a rigorous control over the surrounding territory that belonged to them, and over those who lived in its towns and villages.

THE ARCHITECTURE OF THE MYCENAEAN PALACES

Each Mycenaean palace had its own individual features, but all of them shared certain essential elements, most notably the megaron (great hall), which lay at the heart of each palace.[2] In form, it was a development from the megaron house of the Middle Bronze Age, consisting of a main hall with a porch and, usually, a vestibule. The throne of the king stood in the great hall and before it, in the centre of the room, lay a large ceremonial hearth, its size indicating that it had a ritual rather than purely practical function. At Pylos, channels cut into the floor next to the throne have been interpreted as being there for the king to pour libations in honour of the gods. A balcony probably ran around the sides of the hall on the upper level, with a central chimney above the hearth.

The walls of the palace buildings were carefully constructed, with rubble foundations, lower courses of stone and a superstructure of mud-brick set on a framework of wooden beams. Some exterior walls were faced with finely cut ashlar-style blocks of limestone. Building materials were usually local, but at Mycenae, for instance, it is clear that fine stones were imported and carved in relief to decorative effect. Architectural features such as columns and door frames seem to have been made of wood, though there is some evidence also for the occasional use of carved-stone column capitals. The palaces consisted of a network of rooms, corridors and open courtyards, and remains of staircases show that in some areas they reached at least two storeys.

The palaces were highly decorated with brightly coloured frescoes painted on walls and floors.[3] The Mycenaeans learnt the art of fresco painting from the Minoans, who painted scenes onto wet lime plaster, adding further details when dry. A great variety of colours were used: black, white, yellow, blue, green, red, pink, brown, maroon and grey; all of these came from natural mineral and earth sources, except for blue, which was known as 'Egyptian blue' as it was created in Egypt. The Mycenaeans adopted the Minoans' techniques and also their motifs, but they nevertheless developed a style very much their own. These frescoes, although sadly found in a very fragmentary condition, are a rich source of study for the lives of the Mycenaeans.

Some of the frescoes included depictions of buildings, giving us glimpses of the appearance of towns and palaces and of architectural features not visible from the remains on the ground. A detail from a fresco that once decorated the walls of the megaron at Mycenae, for instance, shows a walled city, with black-and-white chequerboard motif indicating ashlar masonry; wooden beams are seen supporting the walls, and the wooden columns are shown to be of Minoan style, tapering down slightly from the top. Also from Mycenae, from the House of the Oil Merchant, are fragments that show ashlar masonry, a window and mortised piers. From Pylos come frescoes of shrines or gateways, with stone piers on either side of the entrance and a central column, their roofs surmounted by antithetical beasts, lions and sphinxes. An early shrine-façade fresco from the same palace includes details such as horns of consecration (stylized bulls' horns), familiar to us from religious contexts on Minoan Crete, and a half-rosette decorative dado panel.

Mycenae

Three great citadels dominated the Argolid in the north-east of the Peloponnese: Mycenae, Tiryns and Midea. The most famous of all Mycenaean citadels, Mycenae itself, was built on a low rocky hill rising some 40 m (131 ft) out of the north-east corner of the Argive plain and protected to the north and south by deep ravines. Vast and imposing walls enclose the palace within, and are largely preserved today.[4]

The rulers of Mycenae in the Shaft Grave Era had lived on an apparently unfortified acropolis; the hill was only fortified in the middle of the fourteenth century. The north and part of the south-east wall of the fortifications (as they stand today) belong to this early wall, which originally followed the line of the limestone rock of the acropolis and onto which its foundation courses were laid. The massive walls were built in the Cyclopean style: large blocks of roughly hewn limestone, quarried from the rock of Mycenae itself, the inner and outer façades filled with rubble and soil to form walls that were more than 8 m (26 ft) thick in some places. At both Mycenae and Tiryns (whose walls were built some twenty-five to thirty years earlier) the blocks of stone were extremely large and polygonal in form. They were fitted closely together to make the most impressive, irregular and imposing areas of the walls of both citadels. Such monumental walls may have been built to defend the palace within, either from an outside threat or from other Mycenaean centres, or were perhaps built to

40. View of Mycenae showing the Lion Gate.

impress and confer great status on the rulers of the sites. They certainly are, even today, awe-inspiring.

Some one hundred years later, around the middle of the thirteenth century, a massive extension of the walls of Mycenae almost doubled the fortified area of the citadel. This took place after a series of destructions at the site, which affected the Oil Merchant group of houses and two of the Panayia houses outside the walls of the citadel. One of the Panayia houses was clearly destroyed by an earthquake in the second half of the thirteenth century (at the end of LHIIIB1), as a woman was found in the ruins, lying in a doorway with her skull crushed. A second house was damaged by the same earthquake but not destroyed, only to burn down some years later. As part of this extensive rebuilding, the west wall was moved some 50–60 m (164–96 ft) down to the foot of the hill and the royal graves of Circle A were brought within the protective orbit of the walls. The inclusion of the early graves within the walls may be indicative of veneration felt by these Mycenaeans of the thirteenth century for their ancestors of some three hundred years earlier, or it was perhaps a way of legitimizing their rule in some way. The walls of this second phase were also built in the Cyclopean style, and where they no longer lay on bedrock were given shallow foundation trenches filled with a layer of small stones and white clay.

To this great building programme of *c*.1250 BC belongs the vast and impressive Lion Gate. This was approached by a great ramp, flanked on the left by the natural rock of the hill (with a façade of conglomerate blocks) and on the right by a rectangular bastion (built again of massive blocks of conglomerate). The Lion Gate itself is truly monumen-

41. View of Mycenae from the south-west.

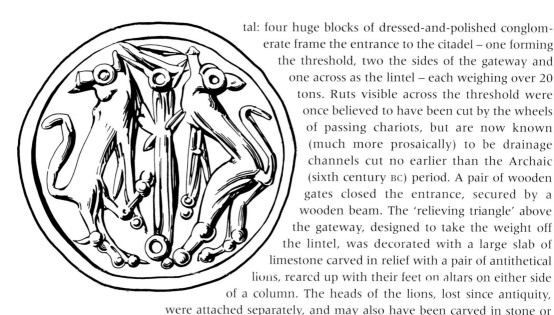

tal: four huge blocks of dressed-and-polished conglomerate frame the entrance to the citadel – one forming the threshold, two the sides of the gateway and one across as the lintel – each weighing over 20 tons. Ruts visible across the threshold were once believed to have been cut by the wheels of passing chariots, but are now known (much more prosaically) to be drainage channels cut no earlier than the Archaic (sixth century BC) period. A pair of wooden gates closed the entrance, secured by a wooden beam. The 'relieving triangle' above the gateway, designed to take the weight off the lintel, was decorated with a large slab of limestone carved in relief with a pair of antithetical lions, reared up with their feet on altars on either side of a column. The heads of the lions, lost since antiquity, were attached separately, and may also have been carved in stone or perhaps made of bronze. These lions may have been the heraldic device of the royal house of Mycenae and are symbolic of great strength and power.

42. Seal-stone made of steatite and carved with a pair of lions, its design perhaps derived from the Lion Gate at Mycenae; from Enkomi, Cyprus.

The palace itself was built on the very summit of the hill, on artificial terraces. Two streets led to it within the citadel walls, one from the Lion Gate and one from the Postern or North Gate, both of which led to a staircase and thence to a small courtyard at the north-east corner of the palace. From here a *propylon* of two porches, each with a central column, gave access to a street into the interior of the palace. At its most extensive, the palace covered an area of more than 300 sq m (2 acres), built on terraces and divided into three sections – north, south and east – by three corridors. Sadly, later occupation of the site and weathering of the rocky and exposed summit on which the palace itself was built have all taken their toll. The north wing, built on the summit, was probably where the ruling family lived, though little remains of it today. In the south section were the megaron and other ceremonial rooms, and in the east were found further rooms of the palace complex.

The megaron was approached via a large and brightly painted courtyard, its thick plaster floor a pattern of red, yellow and blue squares. The megaron (measuring 23 x 11.50 m [75 x 37 ft]) had three rooms, and the visitor had to pass through two entrance rooms before gaining access to the great hall in which the king sat. In the porch, decorated with a triglyph and half-rosette frieze, stood an offering table made of purple limestone, presumably for the visitor to make an initial offering on first arrival. From here a doorway led into the vestibule – again brightly coloured, its stucco floor painted with squares of red, yellow and blue zigzags – which was furnished with low stone

43. OPPOSITE TOP View from inside the walls of Mycenae looking out over the back of the Lion Gate.

44. OPPOSITE Plan of Mycenae and key to main areas.

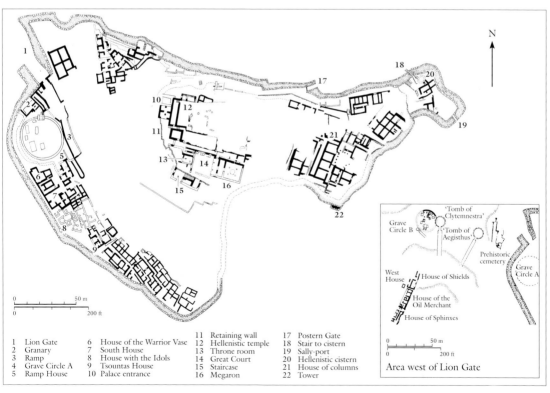

1 Lion Gate
2 Granary
3 Ramp
4 Grave Circle A
5 Ramp House
6 House of the Warrior Vase
7 South House
8 House with the Idols
9 Tsountas House
10 Palace entrance
11 Retaining wall
12 Hellenistic temple
13 Throne room
14 Great Court
15 Staircase
16 Megaron
17 Postern Gate
18 Stair to cistern
19 Sally-port
20 Hellenistic cistern
21 House of columns
22 Tower

Area west of Lion Gate

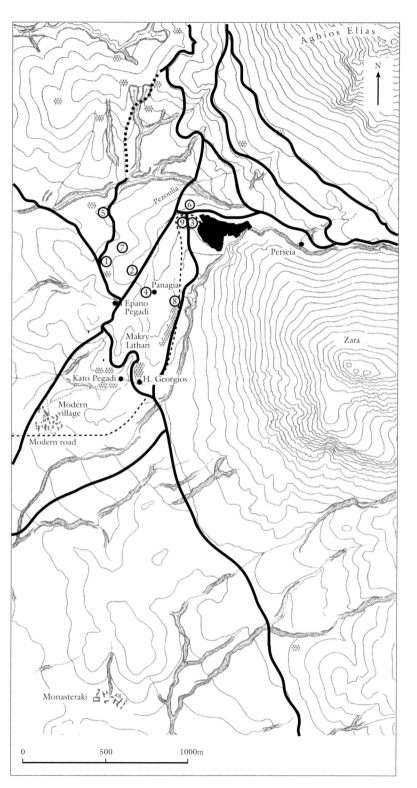

45. Plan of the area around the citadel of Mycenae, including tholos tombs and road system.

Key
1 The Cyclopean Tomb
2 The Epano Phourno
3 The Tomb of Aegisthus
4 The Panayia Tomb
5 The Kato Phournos Tomb
6 The Lion Tomb
7 The Tomb of the Genii
8 The Treasury of Atreus
9 The Tomb of Clytemnestra

benches, presumably for the use of visitors awaiting their audience with the king. The great hall itself measured 12.96 x 11.50 m (42 x 37 ft) and was an imposing structure indeed. In the middle of the room, facing the visitor as they entered, stood the great round ceremonial hearth (3.7 m [12 ft] in diameter) and decorated with a pattern of flames and spirals. Around it were four wooden columns standing on stone bases. To the right of the hearth stood the ceremonial throne itself. Part of the hearth, the king's throne, and two of the megaron walls have long since collapsed into the Khavos ravine, though the floor has been restored.

The megaron was the ceremonial heart of the palace, where the king would have sat in state on his throne receiving visitors, probably both his own people and dignitaries from abroad. For such visitors, the hall at Mycenae would have been tremendously impressive and the fresco paintings on its walls would have left them in no doubt that they were in the presence of a mighty warrior. The preserved west and north walls had been painted with a fresco (about a metre [just over 3 ft] high and probably placed at eye level) depicting a great battle taking place on the walls of the megaron. On it, fragmentary though it is, we see women looking out of the windows as a warrior falls from the walls, horse-drawn chariots hurtling across the landscape and armed warriors fighting in hand-to-hand combat (fig. 48).

The residential quarters of the kings of Mycenae and their families in the north wing have suffered badly from erosion and later building and it is not possible to reconstruct the kind of lives they led in them. Other areas of the palace, though, lower down the slopes of the acropolis, have fared rather better. From the buildings found within the walls it is clear that the palace had areas set aside for religious worship, the workshops of highly skilled craftsmen and the storage of agricultural produce, as the numbers of large *pithoi* (storage jars) and basements containing carbonized cereals and pulses testify.

Outside the walls lay clusters of houses, some of which appear to have had some kind of official status and function, whereas others were apparently simply living quarters. The Mycenae Survey, undertaken in the early 1990s, has studied both the town and the road system in the immediate vicinity of Mycenae.[5] The limits of the town seem to have been established by the late fourteenth century and buildings of both the fourteenth and thirteenth centuries have been revealed. Although only a few isolated pockets of the town have been excavated, it appears that the buildings of the fourteenth century were of rather simpler construction than those of the thirteenth. The latter were more strongly built, often on terraces supported by Cyclopean retaining walls.

Simple residential areas include the three Panayia houses to the east of the citadel, dating to the thirteenth century. Other parts of the town, though, clearly had an official and commercial nature, such as a

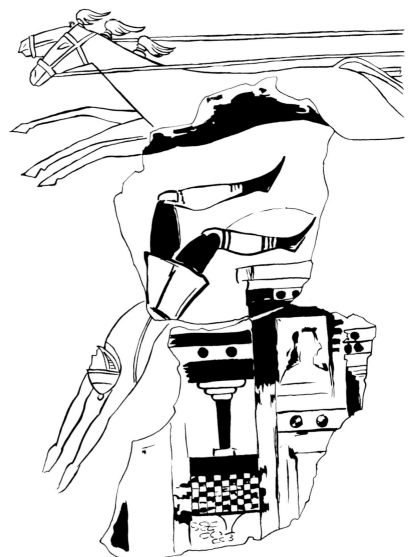

46. LEFT View of Grave Circle A and landscape beyond.

47. LEFT, BELOW The Postern Gate at Mycenae.

48. RIGHT A battle scene painted on the walls of the megaron (great hall) at Mycenae.

complex of buildings close to the Tomb of Clytemnestra, which includes the West House, the House of the Oil Merchant, the House of Shields and the House of Sphinxes. Linear B tablets have been found in four buildings in this complex, showing that the commercial activity taking place there was controlled by the palace bureaucracy. Some of these tablets were written to regulate such activities as the rationing of wool and the collection of spices, whilst another set listed male and female personnel. The West House had a kitchen, which suggests that this was where people organizing the activities in rooms around them were living.

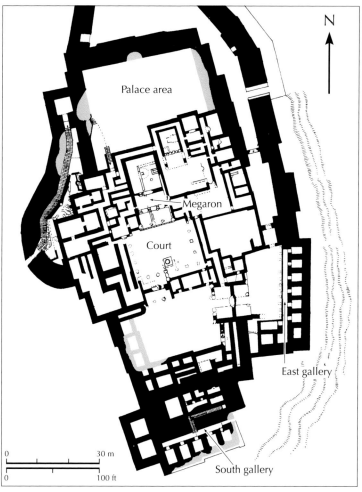

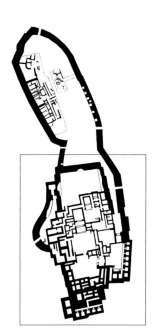

49. Plan of Tiryns.

Tiryns

Lying not far from the great citadel of Mycenae is the fortress of Tiryns, built on a low hill rising 18 m (59 ft) above the Argive plain.[6] In the Bronze Age Tiryns was far closer to the sea than it is today, with the coastline only 300 m (328 yards) to the south-west of it in the Early Bronze Age (around 2,500 BC). By the time the palace was built, though, the sea had receded, leaving Tiryns about 1km (just over half a mile) inland. Tiryns was the first of the Mycenaean citadels to be fortified, some twenty-five to thirty years before Mycenae, in the early years of the fourteenth century. The walls initially enclosed a relatively small area – later occupied by the buildings of the fully fledged palace – and were made of large blocks of stone, laid either directly onto the bedrock or on foundation trenches.

There were three main building phases of the citadel. The first city wall (dating to around 1400–1375 BC) enclosed an area of around

50. View of the galleries built within the walls of Tiryns.

4,690 sq m (just over an acre), and the palatial buildings within its circuit included not one but two megarons. Tiryns grew rapidly in size, but then in the middle of the thirteenth century there were destructions within the citadel. These are contemporary with those that took place at houses at Mycenae and therefore both may well have been caused by the same earthquake. Just as at Mycenae, the walls of Tiryns were rebuilt, and a larger and far stronger wall, with an impressive double gateway, was built around the palace on the upper citadel, almost doubling the fortified area. At the same time, mud-brick walls on stone foundations were built around the lower citadel. A fire led to further rebuilding, and in the second half of the thirteenth century the mud-brick walls were replaced with stone ones, thus enclosing both the lower and upper citadels within strong stone walls. The third and final building phase dates to late in the thirteenth century and is the one that is most clearly visible today. The walls of Tiryns, made of red and grey limestone quarried from nearby hills, were so wide in many areas (from 5 to 11 m [16 to 36 ft]) that great corbelled galleries and rooms were built inside them. They are the finest examples of fortifications anywhere in the Mycenaean world.

These massive walls were approached by a long, steep ramp that led around part of the outside of the fortifications to an entrance in the east wall, through an imposing double gateway. Once within the citadel, the great megaron was reached via a large colonnaded courtyard. The megaron porch, finely decorated with a frieze of alabaster that was carved in relief with half-rosettes and inlaid with blue glass paste, led through the vestibule into the great hall. To the right of the central hearth, against the wall, a raised platform for the king's throne still survives today. The floor of the megaron was coated in stucco and decorated with squares of brightly coloured stylized flowers, octopuses and pairs of dolphins. The complex of rooms around the megaron seem to have been occupied by the ruler and his family and included a large and fine bathroom, its floor a vast monolithic block of stone, measuring some 30 x 40 m (98 x 131 ft) and weighing more than 20 tons. In the north-west corner a channel was cut to drain away the water. A small antechamber that led off from the bathroom was furnished with a stone bench and was probably a changing room.

Little can be reconstructed of the frescoes that once decorated the walls of the palace at Tiryns. Most of the fragments that have survived were not found *in situ* but rather in dumps of material from earlier building phases; these were under the floors of the existing buildings and scattered in courtyards. Those scraps that we do have, though, show that this fine palace with its forbidding fortifications once had buildings beautifully decorated with scenes that included sphinxes, bull-leaping, hunting, a life-size bull, figure-of-eight shields, rockwork and spirals.

The lower town has now been planned using a geophysical survey of the area. At first sight it didn't appear to be particularly large; in fact it seemed even smaller than the town that grew up after the destruction of the palace in the early twelfth century BC. However, the geophysics showed that a large area of the town of the palatial era was flooded and subsequently buried under 4 m (13 ft) of alluvium when the nearby Manessi river changed course and inundated the town. With great engineering skill, the inhabitants were able to build a dam and a canal, which diverted the river away from the town again.

The proximity of Tiryns to Mycenae is puzzling as it seems unlikely that this area of the Argolid could support two fully independent palaces and their dependent territories. It may be that Mycenae exercised some kind of political control over Tiryns and exploited its position near the coast for trading purposes.

Midea

The third of the great fortified citadels of the Argolid is Midea, which lay on the eastern edge of the plain, roughly equidistant from Mycenae to the north-west and Tiryns to the south-west.[7]

Midea was built on a low conical hill rising some 170 m (558 ft) above the Argive plain, with steep slopes and a good view over the surrounding countryside. The summit of the hill was fortified on all sides except for an area on the east and south-east where the precipitous rock provided natural protection. Two gates, one to the east and one to the west, gave access to the acropolis, some 24,000 sq m (almost 6 acres) of which lay within the fortifications. Current excavations at the site have uncovered a large megaron complex (14 x 7.5 m [46 x 24 ft]), unusually constructed not on the summit of the hill itself as in other palaces but rather on a lower terrace. Burials at nearby Dendra – with its tumuli, rich chamber tombs and fine tholos – would seem to point to the presence of a palace within the walls of Midea, and indeed the megaron and its environs have yielded fine masonry, fresco fragments, precious raw materials and finished luxury items. Inscribed sealings have also been found at Midea, showing that it was an administrative centre, but as yet no tablets have been discovered to confirm that it functioned as a palace.

Thus the Argolid continued to be home to a flourishing Mycenaean culture, just as it had been in the Shaft Grave Era. When we head south-west to that other precociously brilliant region of the early Mycenaean years, Messenia, we find a similar sophistication.

Pylos

When we look at the pattern of settlement in Messenia, which in the Shaft Grave Era had been home to several independent chieftains, we see that the situation has changed. In the palatial era (the fourteenth and thirteenth centuries) just one of these sites, that on the low hill of Epano Englianos at Pylos, has outgrown and outshone all the others. This is known as the 'Palace of Nestor' after the legendary king immortalized by Homer as living at 'sandy Pylos'.[8]

The buildings of the Shaft Grave Era on the Epano Englianos hill had been largely destroyed by the levelling of the summit prior to the erection of the thirteenth-century palace. There must also have been fine buildings of the fourteenth century as the excavators found fresco fragments from this phase that would have once have decorated the walls. Two of these fragments are closely related to scenes of Minoan iconography: a bull-leaper, painted in red against a blue ground with long locks of hair and a Minoan-style loincloth and belt, and a daemon with its paw raised to a sacral knot, again a ritual scene familiar from Minoan art. It is therefore possible that Minoan-style rituals were practised at Pylos during the fourteenth century.

The thirteenth-century palace itself was short-lived: it was built

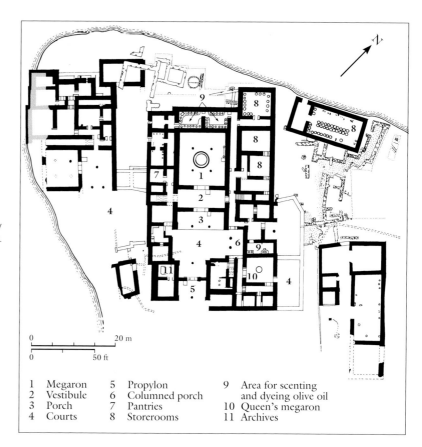

51. Plan of Pylos with key to main areas.

0 ——————— 20 m

0 ——————— 50 ft

1	Megaron	5	Propylon	9	Area for scenting
2	Vestibule	6	Columned porch		and dyeing olive oil
3	Porch	7	Pantries	10	Queen's megaron
4	Courts	8	Storerooms	11	Archives

around 1300 BC and inhabited for about one hundred years, before being destroyed by fire around 1200 BC. The area of the palace was not built over in later years and its ruins lay undisturbed until they were excavated. Thus we are able to get a much better understanding of how the palace at Pylos functioned than we can at say Mycenae and Tiryns, where later structures have damaged the Mycenaean levels of the site. The palace itself covered just over half of the low hill on which it was built, an area of about 85 x 70 m (278 x 229 ft). It lay on a south-west to north-east axis and was arranged in three main units. The most important of these was the central one, which housed the megaron and the palace archives in which were found over a thousand Linear B tablets. The porch and vestibule of the megaron at Pylos both had painted stucco floors and walls adorned with frescoes. On the walls of the vestibule was a processional fresco of figures about 30 cm (almost a foot) high. Most of the figures were male, dressed in kilts or long robes, but at least one was female, wearing a long flounced skirt. A life-size figure of a bull seems also to have formed part of the procession. This frieze was probably painted to symbolize men and women taking part in a procession that was either ritual in honour of a deity or ceremonial in honour of the king. It may even have incorporated both functions if the rulers of Pylos were seen in some way as having a priestly function, as does seem to have been the case in Minoan Crete.

The main hall of the megaron (12.90 x 11.20 m [41 x 36 ft]) had a large central hearth made of clay, which was coated in stucco and decorated with flame and spiral patterns like that at Mycenae. To the right of it stood the throne, with channels in the floor alongside it, presumably for the pouring of libations. The walls of this great hall were richly decorated with frescoes. Behind the throne (of which a low base remains) were heraldically flanking griffins – couchant and wingless – each with a couchant lion behind. A fresco from the eastern corner features a male figure, about one-quarter life-size, bare-headed and wearing a long robe. He is seated on stripy rocks against a red ground and plays a five-stringed lyre. The figure seems to be associated with scenes of much smaller-scale men, who are seated and engaged in some kind of feasting ceremony; a bull, apparently trussed ready for sacrifice, is pictured with them. Perhaps this Pylos bard is singing of the deeds of great warriors, a predecessor of Homer from several hundred years before such poems were finally written down. The floor of the hall was decorated with squares of abstract pattern and, directly in front of the throne, with a large octopus. Found in a room adjacent to the megaron, and thus perhaps from its south-west wall, were fragments of a life-size frieze of deer and papyrus plants.

52. A bard seated on a rock and playing a lyre, painted on a wall of the throne room at Pylos.

53. Griffin and lion fresco from the megaron at Pylos.

The megaron was surrounded by a series of rooms, corridors and stairways. An important group of rooms in the south-east corner of this complex included a bathroom, complete with a fine terracotta bathtub – decorated on the inside with spirals – incorporating a soap-dish; a small step beside the tub was obviously there to help the bather get in (fig. 56).

Storage areas for various commodities important to the Mycenaeans have been identified at Pylos, particularly in the central unit of the palace. North of the main hall, two rooms were used to store perfumed oils; they contained thirty-three large clay *pithoi* and a number of Linear B tablets referring to olive oil and scents for perfuming it. To the west of the megaron, five rooms contained over 6,000 pots. Near the north-east corner of the central unit were two rooms that held over thirty-five wine jars and sixty or more clay sealings, some inscribed with the Linear B ideogram for wine.

Other areas of the palace were used for religious ritual and for workshops. To the right of the central complex lay six rooms linked by a corridor. One of these rooms was open across the front and had a rectangular stone base, which was plastered and decorated. It seems likely that this was a focus of cult at the palace, a suggestion strengthened by the discovery there of a Linear B tablet referring to the goddess 'Potnia Hippeia'. Other rooms of this complex contained fragments of bronze and ivory and Linear B tablets detailing chariot repairs, which indicated that they were palace workshops.

Until recently it was believed that Pylos was an anomaly, in that unlike other Mycenaean palaces it did not appear to have had a fortification wall. A geophysical survey of the area, though, has demonstrated that the size of the site is far greater than had previously been supposed. The palace itself in fact lies at the heart of a large town that stretched out for a kilometre (just over half a mile) along the Englianos ridge, covering an area of around 200,000 to 300,000 sq m (some 50 to 75 acres). Traces of a wall have also been found, 60 m (197 ft) long and up to 2.7 m (almost 9 ft) wide in places, indicating that at least part

54. Throne room in the 'Palace of Nestor' at Pylos.

of the town was fortified. Further investigation of the territory around the palace has shown that the people of Pylos, like those of Tiryns, were skilled at engineering and able to adapt their landscape and water resources. There is evidence that they diverted the nearby Selas river so that it ran through a channel, perhaps to stop it silting up, and that they created a man-made protected port and lake in the vicinity of the palace.

Thebes

The area of modern Boiotia in central Greece was clearly also a great bastion of Mycenaean culture in the years of the fourteenth and thirteenth centuries BC, and the fame of the palace of Thebes in myth and legend rivals that of Mycenae. Travellers to the area in the nineteenth century AD were able to see many ancient remains, but today these lie buried beneath the sprawling modern town. The Mycenaean palace can thus only be excavated in isolated pockets, as redevelopment allows archaeologists access to random plots of land. Although the resulting picture is both incomplete and in some ways confusing, it is increasingly clear that Thebes was once one of the most wealthy and important sites in Mycenaean Greece. Lying in the centre of a fertile plain, its position would have given it control of major routes linking the great Mycenaean centres of Attica and the Peloponnese with areas of central and northern Greece.

The Mycenaean palace was built on the Kadmeia, a low hill now roughly in the centre of the city of Thebes, and appears – as far as one can tell from the piecemeal excavations undertaken so far – to have covered a large area, fortified in the fourteenth century. An important building (around 40 x 18 m [131 x 59 ft]) known as the 'House of Kadmos' after a reference by Pausanias, lies on a north-east by south-west axis and is the most completely preserved of the Mycenaean buildings thus far excavated on the hill. It was decorated with frescoes, including a large one of a procession of life-size women carrying gifts such as flowers and ritual vessels. From the House of Kadmos came objects in precious materials, gold jewellery, rock crystal and agate, and a large number of stirrup-jars, many of which were imported from Khania in west Crete and upon which were painted signs in Linear B script.

Further excavations on the Kadmeia hill (from the 1960s to the present day) have uncovered another palatial building known as the New Kadmeion, this time lying on a different axis, namely north-south. One of its rooms is known as the 'Treasury' because when it was excavated its floor was found to be littered with gold, agate, lapis lazuli, ivories and a cache of Near Eastern cylinder seals, some of which were already heirlooms by the thirteenth century. Other notable buildings now excavated include palace workshops and storage areas, as well as what may have been the palace archive, containing seventeen Linear B tablets, and the 'Arsenal', in which were found bronze weapons, fragments of bronze body armour and the legs of an ivory throne.

The buildings belonging to the palace at Thebes are difficult to interpret. Given the severely hampered excavations, no coherent ground plan can be established and it is therefore hard to make sense of the fact that some of the buildings lie on a north-east by south-west orientation and others on a north-south one. It may be that all the buildings belong to the same palace, making it very large indeed. They may, however, represent two successive phases, with the House of Kadmos (or Old Kadmeion) being destroyed late in the second half of the fourteenth century and immediately being replaced by the New Kadmeion, built on a different axis but reusing some areas of the old palace, such as the 'Arsenal'.

The recent discovery and study of caches of Linear B tablets found in pockets of the site (made accessible by redevelopment of building plots in the modern town) has shed new light on the palace of Thebes and its contacts with nearby settlements.[9] The boundaries of the kingdom controlled by Thebes have still not been fully established, though the mention in the tablets of places called Eleon, Karystos and Amarynthos would seem to indicate that the control of the palace extended over south-eastern Boiotia to incorporate the south of Euboia. The small coastal town of Glipha, on the mainland opposite

55. Two women carrying flowers on a procession fresco from Pylos.

Chalkis, may well have been the port of Thebes. A project (by the Universities of Cambridge and Bradford) to survey the area of southern Boiotia has recently begun and its results should contribute considerably to what we can learn of the territory of the palace.

As to the palace itself, it is greatly to be hoped that current ambitious plans to purchase a number of modern buildings in the centre of Thebes for demolition will allow large-scale excavations at this tremendously important palace to begin, which will then answer at least some of the questions posed by the so far piecemeal investigation of the site.

Orchomenos

Important Mycenaean structures are also to be found elsewhere in Boiotia. The site of Orchomenos was famed in legend as the home of a people called the Minyans, whose wealth was compared by Homer to that of Egyptian Thebes. It was this reputed great wealth that had brought Schliemann there to explore the tholos tomb known as the 'Treasury of Minyas'. This finely built tholos indicates the presence of an important and wealthy settlement site nearby, and in fact the foundations of a building of megaron-form have been discovered next to a Byzantine church near the tholos, its walls once decorated with a battle scene similar to that from the megaron at Mycenae, with fighting warriors and a walled city guarded by sentries.

Gla

Not far away lies the great fortress of Gla, in an isolated spot on a long low hill, standing some 20–40 m (65–131 ft) above the surrounding plain. In Classical times the plain was a lake (Lake Kopais) and the citadel rock of Gla was an island, its walls lapped by water. In Mycenaean times, however, the waters of the lake were drained by a system of dykes – an extraordinary feat of engineering – transforming it into a rich and fertile plain. The hill of Gla appears to have been fortified at the beginning of the thirteenth century, and the fortress remained in use for two generations, suffering destruction and abandonment around 1240 BC. The vast fortification walls enclosed some 200,000 sq m (nearly 50 acres), a far larger area than the Argolid citadels. No palace was found within the walls, but rather a small L-shaped building on an artificial Cyclopean terrace at the northern edge of the hill, which was the main residence and administrative centre for the fortress. Architectural sophistication within the building is seen in the traces of coloured stucco from its walls and floors and the fragments of relief stucco half-columns, some of which were still attached to the walls. Half of a stone 'horns of consecration', so familiar from Minoan sites and found also at Pylos, was discovered in the courtyard, and probably once decorated the roof. South of this building were two long, narrow building complexes. They lay parallel to each other and were of a plan unique to Mycenaean architecture. They were probably used as storerooms and workshops: storage jars and grain residues have been found in them and their storage capacity has been estimated at around 2,000 tons. Large areas of the hill enclosed within the fortification walls appear not to have been built over. The function of Gla thus appears to be different to the other citadels. It was not a fortified palace but rather perhaps part of the fortifications built to protect the great drainage system that had turned the Kopais from a marshy lake into a fertile plain. In addition, it provided storage for produce from the plain and could also, given its great size, be a refuge in times of danger for people and livestock.

Athens

The acropolis of Athens was once home to a Mycenaean citadel, Homer's famed 'great house of Erechtheus', but is now overlain by the great buildings of the Classical period. Some formidable blocks of its great fortification wall (built in the second half of the thirteenth century) can still be seen and a recent study has indicated that the approach into the palace would have had similarities with that to Mycenae, heading west and then north before reaching the gateway. Although the Mycenaean levels on the acropolis at Athens have not been excavated, other sites in the city – such as the agora and the Kerameikos cemetery – give ample evidence for the wealth and importance of Mycenaean Athens.[10]

Iolkos

Traces of Mycenaean palatial buildings at modern Volos on the east coast of Greece have been identified as belonging to Iolkos, the most northerly of the Mycenaean palaces and the place where, as legend has it, Jason and his Argonauts gathered before setting sail on their great voyage into the Black Sea in search of the Golden Fleece. This myth perhaps preserves a memory of the Mycenaeans braving the immense perils of the Black Sea in search of gold, their trading presence there attested by a scatter of Mycenaean pottery sherds along the coastal sites on its shores. An intriguing light has been shed on the palace at Volos with the very recent chance find of a well-built tholos tomb with a fine façade at Kazanaki on the northern outskirts of Volos, together with a nearby built tomb also of Mycenaean date. Interestingly, a Linear B inscription on a stone slab above the relieving triangle of the tomb indicates, with four large signs and three small ones, the number of the burials subsequently found during the excavation of the tomb – namely four adults and three children. The dead were probably all members of the same family, with an initial single burial in the early fourteenth century (LHIIIA1), followed by six more later that same century (LHIIIA2). Just after the palace was destroyed (around 1200 BC) the decayed bodies in the tomb were burned at very high temperatures within the tomb itself, perhaps as some kind of purification ritual after the tragedy that befell the palace.

Lost palaces of legend

Other palaces, believed to exist because their fame is recorded in the poems of Homer, have been sought tirelessly, but with little or no success. Generations of travellers and archaeologists have sought the lost palace of Menelaus and Helen at Sparta, with much of their attention focusing on the Menelaion, a later shrine to them both which has a Mycenaean settlement nearby. Although the site is relatively small and lacks the features of palatial architecture found elsewhere, it is still the most likely centre of regional power in Laconia. Claims (as yet unsubstantiated) have been made more recently for the Mycenaean settlement at Pellana, where the excavator believes he has found the true palace of Menelaus. A similarly determined search has been made on the island of Ithaca for the legendary palace of Odysseus, with a long campaign of excavation at a site at the foot of Mount Aetos (near the modern port of Vathy), where again a Mycenaean settlement has been found, but nothing that can as yet be called a palace. More recently, substantial Mycenaean buildings being excavated on the island of Salamis have been linked with the Homeric hero Ajax, its legendary ruler, but again the structures so far found are not palatial.

FIXTURES, FITTINGS AND FURNITURE

Archaeology gives us what remains of these great and splendid palaces, but time and overbuilding have meant that often what is left are the bare bones of the buildings, with just their foundations to give clues as to their function. How different areas and rooms of these buildings were actually lived in and used by the Mycenaeans is often hard to determine, though items found in them can sometimes give vital clues. Fixtures and fittings built into the fabric of the palaces have sometimes survived *in situ*, most commonly low stone benches that could have served as seats or shelves. Elements that identify rooms as a bathroom have also sometimes survived. At Tiryns the bathroom had wooden walls and a solid stone floor made from a single block; it also had a small antechamber with a stone bench – perhaps a small changing or dressing room. The bathroom at Pylos had a brightly painted terracotta bath tub, complete with a soap dish, and a little step alongside.

Many movable and perishable items must also have made up the furnishings. Simple furniture, such as beds, chairs, stools and tables, would have been constructed from wood and therefore not have survived. Excavators at Thera, using techniques already established at Pompeii, have been pouring plaster into vacuums found in the layers of ash at the site and have recovered the shapes of such pieces of furniture, burnt to cinders by falling volcanic debris. Linear B tablets give us a glimpse of an otherwise almost totally lost category of Mycenaean artefact – the richly decorated furniture of the palaces. The tablets at Pylos list and describe in minute detail the precious items in the storerooms of the palace. Tables made of marble were inlaid with a variety of motifs, such as helmets and seashells, in gold, ivory, rock crystal and blue glass paste. A chair is described as made of ebony with a back of ivory carved with the figure of a man and heifers; and a footstool is inlaid in ivory with a man, a horse, an octopus and a griffin or palm tree. Excavations of tombs and palaces have brought to light carved ivory inlay plaques, which probably once adorned elaborate pieces of furniture; and a pair of carved ivory legs from the palace at Thebes probably once belonged to a special chair or perhaps a throne.

56. Terracotta bath tub in a bathroom at the palace at Pylos.

A thirteenth-century BC workshop for the making of such furniture has been found in the House of the Sphinxes at the town of Mycenae. This building had an area set aside for the assembly of inlaid furniture, and ivory, wood and pumice – the latter for polishing finished pieces – were found in its ruins. Linear B tablets found at the complex to which the House of the Sphinxes belonged show that this area of activity in the town was directly under the control of the palace itself, as one would expect where exotic raw materials were being used. Textiles were probably also used to furnish the homes of the Mycenaeans; one class of textile, known from Linear B as *te-pa*, used so much wool that it must have been some kind of rug.[11]

THE MYCENAEAN KINGDOM

The palaces, richly decorated and often heavily fortified, were the heart of the Mycenaean kingdom, controlling an area of countryside across which were scattered many other settlements of a varying size and importance. The uniformity of Mycenaean culture in the fourteenth and thirteenth centuries shows that these kingdoms, while apparently independent, were nevertheless in close contact with each other.

Recently discovered Linear B tablets from the palace at Thebes have shed further light on contacts between the different regions of the Mycenaean world, and it is to be hoped that as these studies continue, yet more will be learned. One of the new Thebes tablets refers to *ra-ke-da-mo-ni-jo-u-jo*, 'son of Lakedaimon', and others use Lacedaimonian as an adjective, indicating that several Mycenaeans from Laconia are present in the palace. Another tablet listing gifts of grain and olives to various recipients includes the name *e-re-o-ni*, believed to be Eleon, a place in Boiotia referred to by Homer.

Whereas coastal settlements within the Mycenaean world could maintain communication by sea, those inland would have required a system of roads and bridges. In both the Argolid and Messenia, good evidence for road systems has been found. A network of roads linked Mycenae to other Mycenaean centres in the Argolid. On the route to Corinth, retaining walls of Cyclopean masonry were built to support the road as it went along hillsides. Bridges across rivers were constructed with narrow corbelled arches, again in Cyclopean masonry. Good roads would have been needed for effective communications, for overland trade and for the moving of troops. Whilst men travelling by foot or by pack animal could make do with a simple track, more substantial roads would have been needed for carts and chariots.

The great majority of those who peopled the Mycenaean landscape lived in simple houses, usually consisting of a few square rooms grouped together on no particular ground plan. Many of them would have lived in villages and small towns that lay within a territory ruled from a palace. Until recently the main focus of attention has been on the palaces themselves, but now new fieldwork and survey projects have begun to fill out our hitherto rather limited picture of the way the ordinary people lived. The Nemea Valley Archaeological Project has combined archaeological excavation and regional survey to give a clear picture of an ordinary Mycenaean town, Tzoungiza, and its immediate territory. Tzoungiza, its houses clustered together along a ridge, is one of a number of settlements in the Nemean Valley. It grew considerably in the thirteenth century, becoming the main town in the valley, and fine pottery found in the excavations demonstrates that its occupants were fairly wealthy. The town may have grown because of the might of nearby Mycenae, and it is possible that the people of that great citadel extended their power and influence northwards into the Nemean Valley at the time. Less populous areas of the Mycenaean world have also been studied, notably Laconia in the south of the Peloponnese, where the Laconia Rural Sites Project is employing modern scientific methods in its investigation of twenty rural sites in the region.

The archaeological evidence gathered so far paints for us a picture of independent palace centres controlling a territory and the settlements within it, with systems of roads and bridges facilitating communications between different areas within the kingdom. The political realities behind these physical remains – the political geography of the Mycenaean kingdom – is best demonstrated on the mainland of Greece by the archive of Linear B tablets found in the ruins of the palace at Pylos. The evidence of the tablets is complemented in many ways by the work of the Pylos Regional Archaeological Project, which has been surveying the territory in which the palace lies. The tablets reveal that the territory ruled by the palace at Pylos, covering some 2,000 sq km (1,242 sq miles), stretched from the palace itself out to the north as far as Kyparissia and to the east to the foothills of the Taygetos mountains. This territory was apparently divided for administrative purposes into two provinces – 'Hither', meaning 'on this side of', and 'Further', meaning 'beyond' – separated from each other by the Aigaleon mountains. 'Hither' province is believed to refer to the west coast and 'Further' to the valley at the head of the Gulf of Messenia, with the mountain range providing a natural frontier. One of the tablets (In 829) gives a long list of sixteen towns: nine in 'Hither' province and seven in 'Further'. Attempts to identify these ancient names with recognizable sites are fraught with difficulties. One example where this has been attempted is the case of the town *pa-ri-s'*, restored as *(ku)-pa-ri-so*, corresponding to the Classical Greek word for the cypress tree, *kuparissos*. A town with this name, Kyparissia, has existed in the Pylos district since antiquity and was even mentioned in Homer in the form *Kuparisseeis*, but there is no guarantee that they are indeed one and the same place.

In the chapters of this book so far we have traced the evolution of the Mycenaeans' culture and society. We have seen them evolve from their early years to take centre stage in the Aegean and have then followed them as they established complicated and sophisticated palaces and kingdoms at home, exercising far-reaching political control over great swathes of their land. We must now look at how these changes at home are reflected in the relationship of the Mycenaeans with their neighbours in the Mediterranean and with yet more distant lands.

7

Trade and Foreign Relations

The establishment of palace centres across the Mycenaean world in the fourteenth and thirteenth centuries BC intensified the need for exotic raw materials and finished luxury products with which to satisfy the tastes of the palace élites. However, to what extent the Mycenaeans themselves engaged actively in this trade and how much they benefited from the mercantile ventures of other nations is hard to determine. It appears that various trading mechanisms were operating amongst the lands of the Mediterranean: from state-controlled commerce and high-level gift exchange, right down to the smaller-scale activities of groups and individuals.

The Mycenaeans certainly had access to the trade networks active in the east and west Mediterranean; there can be no doubt that goods were being exchanged in both directions. Entrepôts (trading colonies) were established on islands like Rhodes and Kos and at coastal sites like Miletos (on the coast of Asia Minor) to facilitate the processes of trade and exchange yet further. Such activities leave their traces in the archaeological record in a variety of ways: non-Aegean materials found in Mycenaean centres; Mycenaean goods (mostly pottery) discovered in foreign lands; written sources, pictorial evidence and the wrecks of ships that once carried these trade goods found lying on the sea bed.[1]

IMPORTS AT MYCENAEAN SITES

The Mycenaeans, being a Bronze Age people, needed constant supplies of the two metals which when alloyed together make bronze, namely copper and tin. As the palaces were built and the population of Mycenaean Greece apparently grew, the demand for these metals increased. The silver mines at Laurion in Attica, which were also rich in copper, could have satisfied much of the demand for this metal on the Greek mainland; scientific analysis of the copper used in Mycenaean Greece has shown that much of it did indeed come from there. The island of Cyprus was also an important source of copper and supplied large quantities of it to the lands of the eastern Mediterranean. Oxhide ingots of Cypriot copper were widely traded all over the region, as the

57. Oxhide copper ingot from Enkomi, Cyprus.

10 tons of it found on the Ulu Burun shipwreck of around 1300 BC will testify.

When we look for tin in the region, though, the situation is very different. There were no deposits of tin ores either in or near the Aegean or the eastern Mediterranean, so the tin that reached Mycenaean Greece must have come from far distant sources. Suggestions that the Mycenaeans may have acquired tin by trading with Bronze Age Britons for ores from mines in Cornwall in the southwest of England are interesting, but to date, despite intensive fieldwork in the region, archaeologists have thus far found no evidence for exploitation of Cornish tin deposits in the Bronze Age. More convincing perhaps is the suggestion that the seam of tin in Iberia, on the borders of modern Spain and Portugal, may have been a source, as signs of tin-smelting have recently been found there in Bronze Age deposits. Ingots of tin circulating on eastern Mediterranean trade networks, such as the ton of tin found on the Ulu Burun wreck, probably came from sources in the Far East, perhaps Afghanistan, which was also the provenance of the finest lapis lazuli, a prized semi-precious stone found widely in the Bronze Age Aegean.

Likewise, exotic raw materials and finished luxury goods supplied to the wealthy and sophisticated élites of the Mycenaean palaces would have had to be imported. Remains of such goods are found in the ruins of the palaces and tombs and are listed on Linear B tablets, especially those that detailed the contents of palace storerooms where fine pieces of furniture made of precious woods and ivory were kept. The Mycenaeans, given the scale of their demand for metals and luxuries, must have used a variety of trade routes to supply their needs. Gold, semi-precious stones, elephant and hippopotamus ivory and precious woods were imported by sea from the East and from Egypt, for instance, and amber – popular with Mycenaean warriors for their necklaces – came over land routes from the Baltic.

58. Mycenaean stirrup-jars were traded widely for their contents and the shape was copied in Egypt in other materials, such as faience and alabaster. The pottery jar on the right was found at Gurob; the faience one was made in Egypt.

MYCENAEAN EXPORTS FOUND ABROAD

The Mycenaeans must have been trading something in exchange for all these precious goods, of course, and the clearest evidence for Mycenaean exports moving around the Mediterranean – both east and west – is the 'paper-trail' of mass-produced and highly uniform pottery, characteristic of the palace period (fourteenth and thirteenth centuries), which is found abroad.[2] Other archaeologically invisible goods – organic perishables such as textiles for instance – must have been traded, too. Most of the pots were closed shapes such as stirrup-jars and flasks, used to transport liquids. Many of them will have been filled with perfumed olive oil, an industry which is clearly attested in the Linear B tablets from the palace at Pylos. Some vessels, though, were not just containers but highly valued pieces in their own right, notably large Pictorial Style vases painted with lively scenes of people and animals. These were made on the mainland of Greece but are found predominantly in Cyprus and the Near East.

59. Mycenaean Pictorial Style vase decorated with a chariot group and a man carrying what appears to be an oxhide ingot.

60. Mycenaean thirteenth-century *krater* (bowl) decorated with a bull and an egret.

TEXTS

The Linear B tablets discovered to date only document the internal workings of the palace bureaucracies and not their external contacts. It is disappointing that no tablets dealing with trade have been found, though it is possible that some of them may refer indirectly to the kind of gift exchange that we see in operation in the records of the East and Egypt: some high-status items, such as textiles (at Knossos) and perfumed oils (at Pylos), are referred to as *ke-se-nu-wi-ja* (*xenuisa*), which given its similarity to the Classical Greek word *xenos* (which means stranger, host or guest) might indicate they have something to do with gift-giving.

When we look to the eastern Mediterranean, where so much of this trade and gift exchange was carried out, the picture is brought vividly to life by the kinds of documentary evidence that is lacking from Mycenaean Greece. This was a world dominated by three great empires: Egypt, Hatti (the Hittites) and Babylonia. Their dealings with each other and with the smaller independent kingdoms they dominated are illuminated by rich archives. These archives paint a picture for us of the mechanisms of trade in which the Mycenaeans were taking part.

One such archive of correspondence was found in the Egyptian pharaoh Akhenaten's capital city of Amarna on the banks of the Nile in Middle Egypt. Dating to the fourteenth century, these 'Amarna letters' (as they are called) are inscribed on clay tablets (mainly in Akkadian – the *lingua franca* of official diplomatic correspondence in the eastern Mediterranean in the Late Bronze Age) and reveal the complexity of exchange and the important role played by gift-exchange between the rulers of great empires and their subject kings.

The thousands of cuneiform tablets from the kingdom of Ugarit – a great trade centre on the Syro-Palestinian coast – on the other hand, cover a wider spectrum of society and of the trade processes active in the area. The documents were written in various languages, though – like the 'Amarna letters' – the majority of them were in Akkadian. They throw light on many areas of society, not simply on diplomatic relations but on economy and trade. They document trade in high-status goods and also in basic foodstuffs like cereals and olive oil. The amounts of goods traded are also sometimes recorded: one bill of lading for a ship sailing from Ugarit details how much of its cargo of olive oil was bound for each port of destination.

SHIPS AND SHIPWRECKS

We know of four different types of Mycenaean ship – those used for ceremonies, war, trade and fishing – but their depictions on Mycenaean pottery and on seal-stones are too schematic to give an accurate

61. Ship Procession fresco from Akrotiri on Thera.

picture of how they were built and used. Our most detailed record of Aegean ships of the Late Bronze Age comes instead from a miniature fresco from the town of Akrotiri on Thera, and dates to around 1540 BC. The Ship Procession fresco shows a flotilla of large ships in a ceremonial procession, several small fishing boats in a harbour and one cargo ship in full sail (with a square-rigged sail and a central hold for its cargo, on which the sailors are sitting).[3]

Wrecks of cargo ships like the one on the fresco reveal the truly international and cosmopolitan nature of trade in the Mediterranean in the Late Bronze Age. The most spectacular of these discovered to date is undoubtedly the Ulu Burun wreck, a Canaanite ship measuring 15 m (almost 50 ft) long and 5 m (16 ft) wide found off Kaş on the coast of Turkey, which sank around 1300 BC.[4] Its main cargo consisted of 10 tonnes of copper ingots, 1 tonne of tin ingots, terebinth resin, 145 Canaanite jars, 175 turquoise and cobalt-blue glass ingots, and large quantities of Cypriot pottery vessels of various kinds. Smaller cargoes included logs of ebony, ostrich eggs, seals and a scarab from Egypt bearing the name of Nefertiti, raw ivory (elephant and hippopotamus) and objects carved from ivory (like duck-shaped cosmetic boxes), faience vessels, tin vessels, a gold stemmed cup and an Egyptian statuette of a goddess made of gold and bronze. Plant remains found in the wreck have been carefully collected and studied, and included large quantities of pomegranate seeds and figs. Transport jars for olive oil

62. The contents of a tomb at Enkomi on Cyprus (1400–1200 BC), illustrating the trading networks active in the Mediterranean in the Late Bronze Age. Along with Cypriot material the tomb also contained an Egyptian broad collar and glass vessel, Mycenaean pottery, chariot group and jewellery, and cylinder seals from northern Syria.

and wine were also trade items: the terebinth resin which was found in 130 of the jars may have been there to resinate the contents or was being traded for its own properties. Other foodstuffs on the ship were probably for consumption on the voyage, or were the remains of prepared meals, such as charred wheat and barley. The small quantities of coriander and cumin on board may also have been for use in cooking.

Other finds from the ship of a personal or everyday nature were probably the belongings of the crew, such as a variety of bronze tools, cylinder seals, used oil lamps, wooden folding writing boards, and fishing tackle (net weights, bronze fish-hooks and a bronze trident). Two

Mycenaean swords, two seals, spearheads, knives, razors and chisels, amber and glass beads, and small stirrup-jars and cups found on the wreck appear to indicate that two high-ranking Mycenaeans were on board, either as passengers or in some official capacity.

The extraordinary range of items held in the cargo of the Ulu Burun wreck is illuminating: goods from Egypt, the Aegean, Cyprus, Syro-Palestine, Mesopotamia, and even, in the case of amber, ultimately from the Baltic, were being carried. This cargo reveals a trade in both luxury goods and essential raw materials, and the owners of the ship appear to have been travelling the Mediterranean and the Aegean, picking up and selling on items as required.

Two other wrecks from the Mediterranean, both of which went down at the end of the thirteenth century (around 1200 BC), are far less rich and diverse in their cargo. One fairly small Cypriot merchant ship (less than 10 m [32 ft] long) sank off Pont Iria in the gulf of Argos around 1200 BC. It had a limited but mixed cargo of large Cypriot, Cretan and Mycenaean transport vessels: Cypriot *pithoi*, Minoan coarse-ware stirrup-jars and Mycenaean large two-handled jars. The second ship, which sank off Cape Gelidonya on the southern coast of Turkey, was probably a merchant ship from the East (perhaps Syria) with a mixed cargo of personal and trade items, including a cargo of copper consisting of thirty-nine complete ox-hide ingots and several fragments.

By pulling these different forms of evidence together from the mainland itself and from neighbouring lands, we can start to build up a picture of the patterns of trade and exchange between the Mycenaeans and peoples of various lands across the Mediterranean world.

EGYPT

The Mycenaeans' great neighbour to the south-east was Egypt.[5] The Egyptian empire of the pharaohs reached its greatest geographical extent with the conquests of the Eighteenth-Dynasty pharaoh Thutmose III (1470–1425 BC), which brought within Egypt's domain the great lands of Nubia and western Asia. The best evidence for Egypt's involvement in trade in the Mediterranean comes from texts such as the Amarna letters and from wall paintings on Egyptian tombs. The latter reveal that the Egyptians were certainly in direct contact with the Minoans: people labelled as *Keftiu* are seen on tribute scenes painted on the walls of tomb chapels at the site of Egyptian Thebes, in tombs from the time of Hatshepsut (1479–1457 BC) and Amenhotep II (1427–1400 BC). They are identified as Minoans by their dress and by the offerings that they bring as gifts for the pharaoh, including fine vessels of precious metals and elaborately decorated textiles. This pictorial record is reinforced by archaeological evidence – the presence of goods from each country found in the other.

That the *Keftiu* are Minoans is not disputed, but whether the Egyptians refer directly to the Mycenaeans in their texts is a more complicated question to answer. One term that appears in the texts is 'Isles in the Midst of the Great Green' (a term which first appears in the reign of Thutmose III (1470–1425 BC). 'Great Green' (*wadj wer*) may be a general term for the marshy areas of Egypt itself and for the seas to the north, leading some scholars to believe that the 'isles' in the midst of it could be identified with the lands of the Aegean. The other name that appears in the texts, *'hau nebu'*, has not been translated, but was used later on in Ptolemaic times (third to first centuries BC) to refer to Greece. On the Rosetta Stone, for instance (a tri-lingual text with scripts in Greek, demotic and hieroglyphic), the word for 'Greek' ('Hellenikos') is written as *'of hau nebu'* in the section written in Egyptian hieroglyphs. Furthermore, the people referred to in Egyptian texts as *Tanaja* may well be Mycenaeans, as an inscription from Kom el Hetan (see p.112) would seem to indicate.

If the Egyptians were trading with the Mycenaeans, as they did with the Minoans before them, where were the ports along the coast that could be used to trade with these peoples of the north? Memphis must have been a busy port and a wall painting decorating an Egyptian tomb, the tomb of Kenamun, shows a group of foreign traders in foreign ships unloading at an Egyptian port, which is probably Memphis. But for trade with the Aegean, the coast of Egypt offers few convenient natural harbours; perhaps the best of them along the Marmarican coast being the site of Marsa Matruh. Quantities of Mycenaean pottery have been found at Bates Island, just offshore from Marsa Matruh, but they come from what appear to be mainly domes-

63. Ivory cosmetic box in the form of a duck, dating to the fourteenth century BC, found in a tomb at Ialysos, Rhodes.

tic buildings, rather than from a port or harbour context, probably demonstrating secondary use of the pots. The main Late Bronze Age town of Marsa Matruh was, in fact, probably not on this small island but rather on the mainland coast opposite, which is now completely covered by a modern town, presumably built over the ancient harbour.

The fortified settlement of Zawiyet Umm el-Rasham, close to Marsa Matruh on the coast some 300 km (186 miles) west of the Nile Delta, also offered a good natural harbour and is another possible candidate for a convenient port for trade with the Aegean. The fortress there was probably not built initially for trade purposes, but rather to help the Egyptians fight off the threat from their neighbours the Libyans. Once established, though, it would have provided a stronghold and safe harbour for traders plying their wares along that coast, to and from the Aegean and Egypt. The material found there dates to the reign of the Nineteenth Dynasty pharaoh Rameses II (1279–1213 BC) and includes large quantities of Canaanite jars, Aegean coarse-ware stirrup-jars and fine pottery, including some from the Aegean.

Egyptian tomb paintings portraying *Keftiu* bearing gifts allow us an insight into what kinds of goods from the Aegean were valued in Egypt: textiles, for instance, and vessels of copper and precious metals. Such items may also subsequently have been traded by the Mycenaeans; the Linear B tablets reveal a flourishing textile industry and lists of metal vases are also given in the palace inventories. What we see though in the archaeological record is not these luxury goods, but rather large quantities of Mycenaean pottery. Some forty or so sites in Egypt, from Marsa Matruh in the north to Sesebi in the south, have now produced Mycenaean pottery, most notably perhaps the some 1600 sherds from Tell el-Amarna, short-lived capital of the heretic pharaoh Akhenaten.

If we look back from Egypt to the world of the Mycenaeans we find both luxurious raw materials and finished products that have come from the land of the pharaohs. Some of the finest works of art from the palaces and tombs of the Mycenaeans are made for instance from the ivory (both hippopotamus and elephant) imported from Egypt and worked into finished products (often elaborate cosmetic boxes) by Mycenaean craft-workers.

Could it be though that not just Egyptian products came to the Mycenaeans, but that Egyptians themselves did? Evidence from Linear B hints that this may in fact have been the case: a tablet from Knossos bears the name *ai-ku-pi-ti-jo* (Aiguptios), which means 'the Egyptian'. Furthermore, it has been suggested that under the pharaoh Amenhotep III (1390–1352 BC) a formal diplomatic mission was sent from Egypt to the Aegean to visit the rulers of Crete and some of the Mycenaean kingdoms. The source is an inscription found at Kom el Hetan, a mortuary temple to Amenhotep III that was built near the Valley of the Kings at ancient Thebes. Five statue bases found at the back of the temple had been inscribed with place-names, the fifth of which was the so-called 'Aegean list'. On it, the names *Tanaja* (arguably the Egyptian name for the Mycenaeans) and *Keftiu* appear, perhaps as headers for names of specific places on Crete and in Greece which then follow. The sites appear to be listed in order, as if the inscription is giving an itinerary of an actual journey made by emissaries of the pharaoh. The sites visited were Amnisos, Phaistos, Kydonia, Mycenae, Boiotian Thebes or Kato Zakro, Methana (Argolid), Messana (Pylos, Messenia), Nauplion, Kythera, Ilios (Troy), Knossos, Amnisos (again) and Lyktos.

If we look to the sites listed as receiving the mission, can we find any corroboration in the archaeological record of its having actually taken place? Nine faience plaques bearing the cartouche of Amenhotep III were found at Mycenae and some small items like a faience monkey at Tiryns, but these could just as easily have reached Greece as traded Egyptian trinkets (like those found on the Ulu Burun wreck). Whether or not the Kom el Hetan base does record an actual journey, it still demonstrates that the Egyptians were aware of the important ports and towns in Crete and Greece.

THE EAST

Mycenaean access to trade with the East was clearly vital to ensure supplies of metals and luxuries.[6] Settlements such as those on the islands of Rhodes and Kos, invaluable stepping-stones to the East, grew and flourished. On Cyprus, at the crossroads of trading routes both north-south and east-west, large quantities of Mycenaean pottery have been found, imported from the mainland. The coast of Asia Minor – Ephesos, for example, and Iasos – received imports of Mycenaean pottery, as did Troy to the north and sites in Lycia to the south. At Miletos and Musgebi, which had both Mycenaean pottery and cemeteries of chamber tombs, there may well have been Mycenaean settlers actively engaged in promoting trade. Ongoing excavations at Miletos are uncovering increasing and exciting evidence for a Mycenaean trading entrepôt having been established there at the site of an earlier Minoan colony.

On the Syro-Palestinian coast more sites than ever before have Mycenaean imports, with pottery reaching places like Tell Atchana on the River Orontes, Tell el Hawam, Beth Shan and the port of Tell el Ajul.

Canaanite (or Syro-Palestinian) jars – large transport amphorae about 50 cm (20 in) high, are testimony to the trade between the Aegean and Syro-Palestinian centres in the fourteenth and thirteenth centuries. Ships laden with cargoes of these jars left Ugarit full of wine, oil or resin (or resinated wine and oil). They travelled to the Aegean, selling their cargo on trade routes that stopped at Crete, the Argolid,

64. One of the lions guarding the entry to the Hittite capital Hattusa at Boghazkoy.

Attica, Messenia, Cyprus, and south to Egypt. It seems likely that exotic wines from the East, some of them flavoured with resins, were in fashion and this trade was supplying a market for them in the cosmopolitan centres of the Mediterranean.

At Ugarit, an important trading centre strategically placed to take advantage of sea and land routes, archaeological evidence and archives of texts combine to give a particularly clear picture of trade in the region in the Late Bronze Age. Excavations at Ugarit – which comprises the tell site of Ras Shamra, the port Minet el-Beida and the royal palace of Ras Ibn Hani – have uncovered quantities of texts (mostly written in Akkadian), which bring vividly to life the diplomatic and economic history of the region from the mid-fourteenth to the early twelfth century. No direct correspondence between the Greeks and the rulers of Ugarit has been found, but contacts between the two regions can be traced in the great quantities of Mycenaean pottery that has been found at Ugarit, dating from the early fourteenth century (LHI–IIA1) onwards. At first these pots were imported from production centres on the Greek mainland itself, but later on – in the second half of the thirteenth and early twelfth centuries – they are coming from other sources, notably from Mycenaean colonies that had been established on the islands of Rhodes and Kos. The pottery is a visible trace of the goods being traded, but there must also have been perishables that leave no trace in the archaeological record.

Back in Mycenaean Greece itself, the most spectacular evidence for links between the Mycenaeans and the peoples of Mesopotamia is in the cache of thirty-nine cylinder seals – made from faience, stone and lapis lazuli – found at the palace of Thebes in Boiotia, nineteen of which are imports from Mesopotamia. They range in date from c. 2500 BC to the thirteenth century BC, and seventeen of the nineteen are made of lapis lazuli. The significance of this discovery and the meaning of the presence of the seals at Thebes have been hotly debated and suggestions and theories abound. Were they a collector's hoard? Did they constitute simply a cache of lapis lazuli waiting to be reworked? Were they a diplomatic gift? More common Mesopotamian imports found in Mycenaean contexts are beads and moulded glass objects which were most probably trinkets.

Looking further inland into the heartland of Anatolia, we find the great empire of the Hittites, which had its capital, Hattusa, at Boghazkoy and was one of the great powers (the Hatti) known to us from the 'Amarna letters'. It seems likely that the country named Ahhijawa in Hittite texts is actually Mycenaean Greece, and that therefore we can try and chart the relationship between the two from the records. One of the apparent anomalies in the trading systems of the Late Bronze Age is the marked paucity of evidence for trade links between the two lands. This has led to the suggestion that there was a trade embargo in place. Interestingly, a thirteenth-century Hittite text is inscribed with a treaty – signed between the Hittite king Tudhalija IV and Sausgamuwa of Amarru – which talks of an embargo on the Assyrian king Tikulti-Niurta I, forbidding ships of the Ahhijawa to reach him (see p.197).

THE WEST AND THE NORTH

To the west, Mycenaean pottery has been found on the island of Malta, at Montoro on the coast of eastern Spain, at many sites in south-east Italy and Sicily, and even as far north as the Po Valley. Some sites in Sicily and south-east Italy have very high concentrations of Mycenaean material, for instance in the tombs at Thapsos. In the thirteenth and twelfth centuries such southern sites as Scoglio del Tonno (Taranto) were found to have not only quantities of imports, but also local imitations of Aegean wares. At Broglio di Trebisacce in Calabria the local Aegean wares are of such high quality that they may have been made by Aegean potters living in the area. The scattering of Aegean-style sherds in northern and central Italy – for instance at Fondo Paviani in the north-east and at Luni sill Mignone, Monte Rovello and Ben Giovenale in southern Etruria – may either be true imports or perhaps again the work of local potters. On the island of Sardinia imported Aegean pottery from the thirteenth century has been found at several sites, for instance at Barumini, at a site near to Orosei on the east coast and at Nuraghe Antigori, where the excavators have found quantities of Aegean pottery imported from the Peloponnese and Crete, as well as imitations made by local potters. Ox-hide ingots have also been found in Sardinia and the island may well have played a role in the metals trade in the Mediterranean. Few objects of apparently Italian provenance have been discovered at Mycenaean sites, a notable exception being a winged-axe mould from the House of the Oil Merchant at Mycenae, of the thirteenth century. This stone mould was for the making of bronze axes of a form common in north Italy.

Lands to the immediate north of the Mycenaean world – Thrace, for instance, and modern-day Albania – received Mycenaean imports: Mycenaean swords were particularly prized by the warrior chieftains of those regions.[7] Further to the north, though, the extent of Mycenaean trading links with the lands of northern Europe are obscure. Imports of amber from the Baltic, prevalent during the Shaft Grave Era, are far fewer in the fourteenth and thirteenth centuries, and if copper was being traded from the north down into the Aegean at this time – as many have suggested – there is little Mycenaean pottery to attest to this trade. High-status prestige items, such as gold cups of Aegean appearance, have been found in lands to the north, but their true origin and the mechanisms by which they reached their destination are still a matter for debate.

8

The Lives of the Mycenaeans

From the settlements, tombs, artefacts and written records they left behind them, we can attempt to piece together an impression of the people we call 'Mycenaeans'. The discovery, decipherment and subsequent reading of the Linear B tablets has shed a whole new light on their lives, at least during the time of their palaces which is when the tablets date from. The earliest administrative tablets inscribed with Linear B found so far are those from the Room of the Chariot Tablets at Knossos, dating to LMII (1450–1400 BC). Apart from some examples dating to the fourteenth century BC (LHIIIA), which had been thrown away at Pylos, the earliest from the mainland come from Thebes and from the House of the Oil Merchant complex at Mycenae, dating to around 1350 BC (the end of LHIIIB1). The tablets have revealed that the Mycenaean palace was not simply the home of a warrior king, but also the hub of a kingdom meticulously controlled and ordered down to the smallest detail; a complex bureaucracy was at work. Caches of recently discovered and deciphered tablets from the palace at Thebes have added greatly to this picture, even hinting at connections between the great kingdoms of the Mycenaeans. The painstaking records of the palaces reveal that the society of the Mycenaeans was extremely hierarchical, from the king down to the slaves.

THE KING AND HIS COURT

Most of our information for the workings of a Mycenaean palace on the mainland comes from the archive of the 'Palace of Nestor' at Pylos in Messenia.[1] Tablets found at other palace centres, such as Thebes and Mycenae, seem to indicate that they were organized along similar lines, although still exhibiting local differences.

The Mycenaeans called the ruler of their kingdom the *wanax* (*wa-na-ka* in the syllabic script on the Linear B tablets), a word meaning king and one familiar to us from Homeric epic. From the tablets we understand that the *wanax* was not only the ruler of the kingdom but sometimes also presided over religious rituals, so he may perhaps have been a priest-king – both the political and religious leader of his kingdom and its subjects. To what extent the Mycenaean kingdom was fully under the control of the king and his court is difficult to determine as the tablets do not concern themselves with the issue of political control. Therefore we need to look at other categories of information, such as how the palace and the kingdom functioned economically, to see if the role of the *wanax* can be more fully explained. The tablets concerned with taxation, industry, raw materials and agriculture show that the palace functioned as a redistribution centre. Each palace would have had dependent villages and people within their territories that produced goods of various kinds, which were then collected and stored centrally in the palace. These were then redistributed either as raw materials or, where appropriate, as worked items. All the elements were closely controlled by the palace, and the tablets that regulate these processes show that the palace did indeed exercise a fairly rigorous control over the surrounding territory.

It is clear from the tablets found at Pylos, dating to the destruction of the palace around 1200 BC, that the *wanax* was extremely wealthy in that he owned great estates of land. Although the *wanax* at Pylos is never directly named in the tablets, a man called Enkhelyawon (*E-ke-ra-wo*) is demonstrated by the archives to have been of such high status that it seems reasonable to identify him as the king. Enkhelyawon owned a very large estate of rich agricultural land, which was planted with over a thousand grapevines and as many fig trees. The *wanax* also had personal craftsmen working for him, designated as royal by the term *wa-na-ka-te-ro/ra*. There is a royal potter listed as working at Pylos, for example. Similarly, in the Linear B tablets from the palace of Knossos on Crete, we find references to textiles as being 'royal', presumably a special kind of cloth that was only owned and worn by the king. We also find the term *basileus* on the tablets, which in Classical Greek was used to mean king, but in Mycenaean Greek (as in Homeric epic) it seems to denote a lesser status, equating perhaps to the term chieftain – the head of a group of people rather than of an entire kingdom.

The palace was also home to the members of the court, and the titles of some of these upper echelons of Mycenaean society are also recorded in the tablets. Second in importance to the *wanax* was apparently the *lawegetas*, a term found at both Pylos and Knossos. It is difficult to determine his precise role within the kingdom, though it's possible that he was the head of the army; the term *lawagetas* means loosely 'Leader of the People', and 'people' in Homeric and later Greek usage could have a military aspect.

More certainly connected with the military are the *heqetai* (*e-qe-ta*), which means 'Followers', and certain clues are found in the tablets which can be pieced together to build up a picture of their character and status in society. They were probably an aristocratic élite, who were the companions of the king. The Mycenaeans who are referred to by name on the tablets are usually identified simply by their first

65. Mycenaean Pictorial Style vase decorated with a man between a pair of horse-drawn chariots.

name. The *heqetai* on the Pylos tablets, though, are also given their father's name, perhaps a reflection of their aristocratic status. They are recorded as owning slaves and as having a special kind of cloth made for them, presumably for some kind of outfit or uniform that only they were allowed to wear. Their military status is further implied by the fact that an adjective derived from their title is applied to chariot wheels stored in the palace, suggesting that they owned or used chariots. Furthermore, in the Pylos tablets they are named as the commanders of those who watch the coast – an important job at Pylos, which lay vulnerable to attack from the sea.

WARFARE

The presence of an important and influential military aristocracy forming the upper echelons of Mycenaean society was to be expected from the material remains, which give the overwhelming impression of a fierce and warlike people who gloried in battle and in the hunt. The warrior burials of the Mycenaeans, seen from the sixteenth century onwards, continue throughout the centuries of the palace era and through to the end of the period in the twelfth century. This impression of militarism is further reinforced by the settlement evidence provided by the fortresses and palaces of the Mycenaeans.

66. Warrior and grooms preparing for battle on a fresco painted on a wall of the megaron at Mycenae.

The great and rugged citadels built to protect many of their palaces give an immediate impression of strength and power; an impression conveyed, too, by the fresco paintings that decorated the walls within. A mighty battle was depicted on the walls of the megaron at Mycenae, while in another scene grooms and a warrior are preparing for battle, the latter dressed in tunic, greaves and boar's-tusk helmet (see fig. 66 above). Hall 64 at Pylos was painted with a town built of ashlar masonry and with two warriors similarly wearing linen tunics and boar's-tusk helmets, one riding in a horse-drawn chariot and the other walking behind. There are also striking duelling scenes from Pylos, with Mycenaean warriors in hand-to-hand combat with a variety of enemies, often distinguished by their strange attire, perhaps meant to denote foreigners. In one such battle, Mycenaean warriors, dressed in short white kilts, helmets and greaves and armed with short swords or daggers, are fighting against enemies with shaggy hair who are wearing animal skins knotted at the shoulder. It seems that scenes of battle were considered the most suitable theme for the great hall of the king, reflecting his military prowess and intended to impress his subjects and his visitors.

From a variety of types of evidence we are able to gain a very clear picture of how a Mycenaean warrior was equipped for battle.[2] Perhaps the most immediately identifiable piece of Mycenaean armour is the boar's-tusk helmet, which has been found in tombs spanning the entire Mycenaean period and is known from many depictions of warriors in Mycenaean art. It consisted of a felt-lined leather cap, with several rows of cut boar's tusk sewn onto it. Fifty or sixty tusks were needed to make such a helmet and it was clearly the high-status helmet of the Mycenaeans. Other types in less durable materials have not

67. Ivory head of a warrior wearing a boar's-tusk helmet, thirteenth century BC, from a chamber tomb at Mycenae.

68. The 'Warrior Vase' from Mycenae.

69. The 'Dendra Panoply'.

survived but are known to us from art, such as the horned helmet (worn by soldiers seen marching on the 'Warrior Vase' from Mycenae) and the zoned helmet (which appears to have been made of strips of leather sewn together). A helmet worn by warriors on one of the Pylos frescoes seems to incorporate a nose guard, a feature not otherwise seen on a Greek helmet until the metal Corinthian helmet of Classical times.

Protective body armour of a variety of kinds was also worn by Mycenaean warriors, both in battle and during the hunt. Metal body armour was found dating to as early as the sixteenth century in the shaft graves of Mycenae, but these thin sheet-gold breast-plates were too fragile to have been worn in battle and must have been purely decorative, made for ceremonial occasions or perhaps specially for the funeral. That the Mycenaeans wore more substantial metal armour is made clear by the 'Dendra Panoply' – an impressive corslet made from sheets of bronze, with large shoulder guards and a neck guard – found in a chamber tomb along with a boar's-tusk helmet with metal ear guards. The Dendra Panoply (dating to the late fifteenth/early fourteenth century) dramatically brings to life ideograms on the Linear B tablets: at Knossos a series of tablets recording body armour include an ideogram with a profile very like that of the Dendra Panoply; as do several from Pylos, which are linked with the word *thorax*, the Classical Greek term for a corslet. Occasional finds of small metal scales in tombs suggest that the Mycenaeans also had suits of scale-metal armour, known from the contemporary Near East. Body armour of perishable materials was also worn: warriors fighting or riding to battle on the fresco paintings are often lightly clad, for instance in kilts and bare-chested, or in white linen tunics reaching down to mid-thigh and with short sleeves. Armour made up of several layers of linen could provide quite good protection, but would not easily survive in the archaeological record. A piece of thick material made up of many layers of linen from one of the Mycenae shaft graves may well be a rare remnant of such armour. The Mycenaeans probably also had leather armour, which again would not have survived. Both the linen and leather armour, however, could be reinforced with metal, and traces of such reinforcements have sometimes been identified in tombs. A Linear B tablet from Knossos refers to fine linen for a tunic and to tunic fittings of bronze, indicating a linen tunic reinforced with metal.

Mycenaean warriors and hunters on many of the frescoes wear greaves protecting their lower legs; a few bronze ones have survived in tombs, but none to date have been identified on the Linear B tablets. Shields are also apparently not recorded on the tablets, unless the ideogram for them has not yet been recognized, and have not survived in tombs as they were usually made of perishable materials. They do survive in art though. Large body shields, the figure-of-eight shield and a tall rectangular one (known as the tower shield) are carried by

70. Mycenaean swords and daggers made of bronze and demonstrating a variety of forms.

hunters on the sixteenth-century lion hunt dagger from Mycenae, for instance. Rows of figure-of-eight shields, used as a decorative motif on frescoes, show that they were made of ox-hide. The tower shields carried by Mycenaeans on a miniature fresco from Akrotiri on Thera are clearly made of the same material. Later the Mycenaeans adopted a smaller shield, seen carried by warriors on the Warrior Vase and Warrior Stele from Mycenae and on several late Pictorial Style vases.

The Mycenaean warrior was also armed with an array of weapons. Large numbers of bronze swords were placed in warrior burials, some of them simple examples in bronze and others with embellishments such as sheet-gold hilts, marble or ivory pommels and decorated blades. Two types of long sword (rapiers) were in use from early Mycenaean times. One, Type A, probably of Minoan origin, had rounded shoulders, a short tang and a mid-rib down the length of its narrow blade. The other, Type B, which perhaps originated in the Near East, was a stronger weapon: it had a slightly shorter blade, square shoulders and a longer tang, thus attaching the blade more securely to the hilt. In the fourteenth century, Type A evolved into the cruciform sword and Type B into one with horned shoulders. The Mycenaeans would have used such rapiers for cut-and-thrust fighting. In the second half of the fourteenth century a new type of sword was introduced, probably from the Near East, with a shorter blade with no mid-rib and with a double cutting edge. This was a slashing weapon, and with its introduction must have come a new form of fighting. Warriors fighting each other with such swords are seen on frescoes, notably on the battle scene from Hall 64 at the palace of Pylos.

71. Mycenaean bronze spearheads.

The ideogram for the sword on Linear B tablets is immediately recognizable, but is so schematic as to make it often difficult to distinguish types. On one tablet from Knossos (Ra 1540) a weapon with a mid-rib is shown, but may be either a sword or a dagger. The latter was also an important part of the Mycenaean warrior's array of weaponry and could be a simple bronze one or a very ornamental example; particularly striking are those inlaid with scenes in precious metals, found in tombs of the Shaft Grave Era.

Thrusting spears are held by both hunters and warriors in fresco paintings, and spearheads are found frequently in warrior graves. A lighter spear, like a javelin, also seems to have been used for hunting, but evidence for its use in bat-

72. Mycenaean bronze arrowheads.

tle – so graphically described by Homer – is lacking. Early Mycenaean spearheads had a double-socketed blade fixed onto a split shaft, to be succeeded by a leaf-shaped blade with a mid-rib that was fixed to a wooden shaft by a socket. Arrowheads, made initially of flint and obsidian and later also of bronze, have been found in tombs and are illustrated by ideograms on Linear B tablets. We see bows and arrows used for both hunting and war, such as by the archer on the lion hunt dagger and as carried by Mycenaeans on Pictorial Style vases.

The many representations of Mycenaeans fighting show they did so on foot, but did they also fight from chariots?[3] Chariots appear for the first time in Greece in the art of the Shaft Grave Era, carved in relief on stelai placed above the tombs. Numerous Mycenaean Pictorial Style vases depict them, and terracotta models of chariot groups are often found in tombs. They were perhaps introduced to Greece from Syria/Palestine via Crete. These chariots were fast two-wheeled vehicles with a rectangular chariot box. Shortly before the fall of the palaces at the end of the thirteenth century, a new type of even lighter faster chariot was apparently developed in Greece. Mycenaean art certainly suggests that chariots were used for processions and hunting, despite the rocky landscape of Greece. Enough depictions survive to make it seem likely that the Mycenaeans also used them in battle, as did the people of the Near East and Egypt.

73. Mycenaean Pictorial Style vase decorated with archers, thirteenth century BC, from Enkomi, Cyprus.

74. Terracotta chariot groups. The one on the left is from Ialysos, Rhodes, and the one on the right is from Enkomi, Cyprus.

75. A pictorial papyrus from Tell el-Amarna, Egypt, depicting people in what may be Mycenaean armour and helmets fighting as part of the pharaoh's army.

The warlike nature of Mycenaean society must have been a factor in their relations with other cultures. We have seen them armed and marching on a fresco from the island of Thera (from around 1540 BC) and have looked at the evidence for them taking control of Crete around 1450 BC. Other hints of rather less than friendly relations with other areas are to be found in Linear B tablets: some women listed in the palace records are qualified by the term for 'captives' and were presumably women captured in raids and then taken back to the palaces as slaves.

Mycenaean warriors may also have hired out their services to fight as mercenaries in the armies of foreign powers, such as Egypt. A very fragmentary battle scene, painted on papyrus and showing Egyptian foot-soldiers fighting Libyans, was excavated in 1936 at the site of Tell el-Amarna, capital of the heretic pharaoh Akhenaten (fig. 75). Amongst the two rows of running troops are warriors wearing helmets and ox-hide tunics otherwise unattested on depictions of Egyptian battles. The colour and demarcations of the helmets, the tunics of ox-hide with metal reinforcements and the skin colour and facial features of the warriors arguably identify them as Mycenaeans.[4]

HUNTING

Hunting was clearly seen as a suitable pursuit for the Mycenaean warrior élite: the hunting of wild and dangerous animals would have called upon similar skills and courage as engaging in battle and would have demanded similar equipment. The dangers of the sport are seen on the lion hunt dagger, where one of the hunters is depicted lying beneath the front paws of a lion. Fresco paintings show the Mycenaeans hunting deer and wild boar, the latter important not only for its meat but for its tusks. From Tiryns comes a wonderfully lively fresco of a boar hunt, sadly found not *in situ* but in fragments in a rubbish dump on the west slope of the site. Hunters in short tunics and greaves or leggings take their dogs in pursuit of wild boar. On one fragment spotted hunting dogs wearing red collars surround a boar which is being speared between the eyes by a huntsman. Accompanying the hunters are women riding in chariots, presumably spectators to the sport.

Another hunting scene, this time from Pylos, shows men hunting deer against a landscape through which flows a river; other male figures, accompanied by extraordinarily large dogs, are carrying large tripod cauldrons, presumably for cooking the meat once the deer are caught. Mycenaean Pictorial Style vases also show dogs, with one fine example depicting a man with a pair of lively dogs on leads leaping around him. Domesticated hunting dogs were thus clearly an integral part of the Mycenaean hunt and this is reflected in the Linear B texts, where the word for hunter is *kunagetai* – 'dog-leader'.

76. Hunting dogs chasing a wild boar on a hunt fresco from Tiryns.

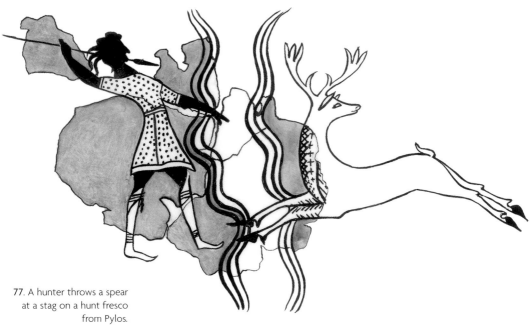

77. A hunter throws a spear at a stag on a hunt fresco from Pylos.

78. Mycenaean Pictorial Style vase, thirteenth century BC, from Klavidia, Cyprus. It shows a man with a pair of dogs on leads leaping up at him and a bull to the left.

WOMEN

Women, presumably high-born or connected to the family of a rich and powerful man, are pictured on the frescoes from the palaces as spectators of warfare and the hunt: at Tiryns they ride in chariots to watch the hunting of wild boar; and at Mycenae they anxiously survey the battle raging outside from the safety of the town. There is no mention, though, on the Linear B tablets of a queen. All of the high-ranking officials in Mycenaean society were male, as far as one can tell from the evidence of the tablets. The only women who appear to have high status in their own right are those who are probably priestesses. One woman, called Karpathia, is listed on a land-holding tablet for the district of Sphagianes (part of the Pylian kingdom) as owning two plots of land, an indication of her wealth and high status. She has the title of 'key- bearer' and is likely to be a priestess, though nothing else is known of her.

The role of women in a society is not only defined by profession, of course, and it is clear that the Mycenaean world is no exception to this. Women of all classes in Mycenaean Greece must have played an important part in various rituals, both religious and funerary. This is seen on a grand scale in the processional frescoes that decorated the walls of the Mycenaean palaces, where richly dressed women carrying gifts are taking part (see fig. 55). On a more personal level, women were involved with funerary rites. The rituals which took place at a Mycenaean funeral are most vividly depicted on painted *larnakes*

79. Women riding in a chariot to watch the hunt on a fresco from Tiryns.

(coffins) from a chamber tomb cemetery at Tanagra in Boiotia (see p.168). These show processions of women, their hands held up to their heads in a gesture of mourning. There are also depictions of the *prothesis*, the laying out of the corpse, and here again it is the women who are caring for the deceased. Some of the women have red drops painted on their faces, perhaps indicating drops of blood from scratching themselves in grief. All these details correspond with later Greek funerary practice.

The women painted on the walls of the palaces can clearly command the finest and most elaborate textiles and rich clothing. Figurines and seal-stones show that the basic form of Mycenaean dress is a long

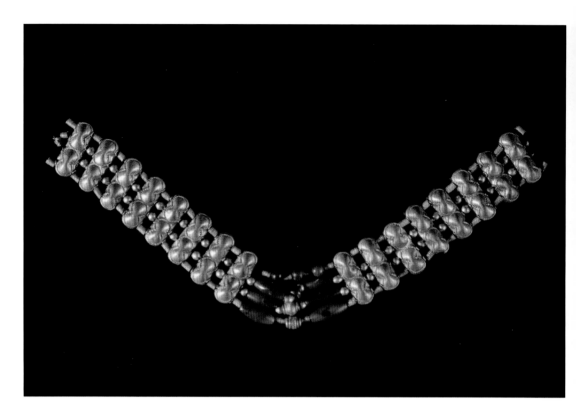

80. Cypriot necklace from Enkomi, Cyprus. Its beads are in the form of the Aegean figure-of-eight shield.

81. OPPOSITE Gold shroud ornaments (below), a necklace made of blue glass beads which were wrapped in gold (above), blue glass locks of hair and beads of rock crystal, amethyst and carnelian (centre).

tunic, usually belted at the waist, sometimes covered by a knitted shawl. Frescoes depict women dressed in a variety of different outfits made from brightly coloured cloth (sometimes patterned), their gowns frequently trimmed with highly decorative embroidered brocade. Tight bodices and long flounced skirts are often accompanied by a shawl worn over the shoulders. Apparently heavy cloaks are also seen, some tied at the shoulder, with fringed edges that appear to indicate that they are of a textured fabric. These garments were made from wool and linen and perhaps also from wild silk. The women's hair is shown plaited or twisted into a number of long tresses, with a fringe and sometimes curls at the front.

The jewellery they wore, known from frescoes and tombs, included necklaces, bracelets, armlets, ankle-rings, finger-rings, hair-rings and earrings. Semi-precious stones were used for beads (amethyst, carnelian, lapis lazuli, onyx, red jasper, sardonyx and chalcedony) and silver and gold were made into exquisite items using techniques like granulation, *cloisonné*, *repoussé* and filigree. These were elaborate pieces of jewellery created with labour-intensive techniques and precious and expensive materials and must have therefore been available to only a very few women at the top of the Mycenaean social hierarchy. In the fourteenth and thirteenth centuries, though, new techniques of jewellery-making were introduced, which made necklaces and ornaments

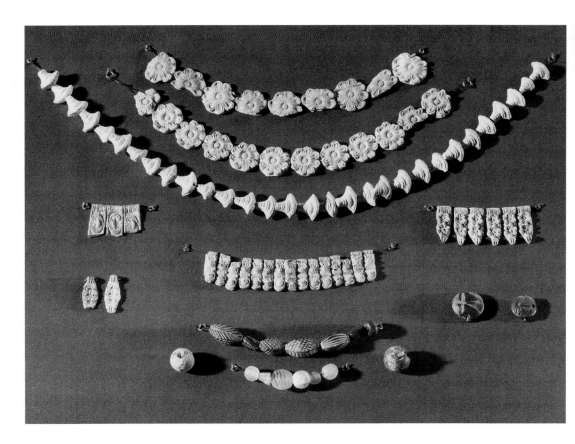

82. TOP Glass beads in a wide variety of shapes produced in moulds made jewellery accessible to more women.

83. ABOVE Ivory hair pin, fourteenth century BC, from a tomb at Ialysos, Rhodes.

available to a wider spectrum of society. Beads of glass and blue paste (*kyanos*) were cast in steatite moulds that were carved on all sides with a variety of bead shapes. These moulds have been found at palaces like Mycenae and Knossos, and were clearly in use in the palace workshops. Their products, though – necklaces of glass beads in the shape of designs like rosettes, lilies, papyrus, palms, seashells and curls of hair – are found all over the Mycenaean world, often in fairly simple burials. Some of these glass beads were carefully wrapped in thin sheet gold to give the appearance of a gold necklace, an early form of gilding. Women were also buried with cosmetic items, such as combs, ivory boxes in the form of ducks and ivory hairpins.

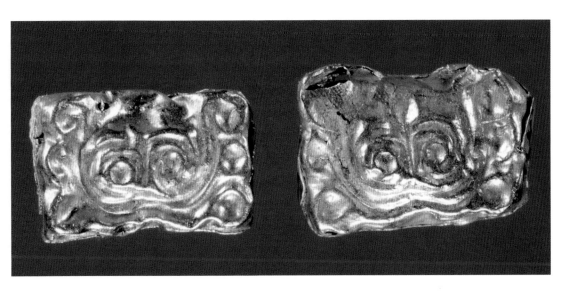

84. Gold shroud ornaments in the form of a stylized octopus.

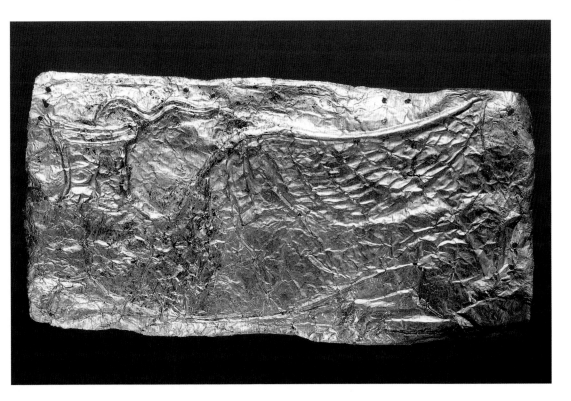

85. Gold plaque (one of four) from Ialysos, Rhodes, decorated with a sphinx in *repoussé*; probably a cover for a wooden box.

86. Intricately carved ivory group of two women (perhaps goddesses) playing with a child, from the north side of the palace at Mycenae.

CHILDREN

The children of the upper echelons of Mycenaean society do not appear in the Linear B tablets, nor do those of the ordinary people; the only children that are mentioned are slave children. Actual depictions of children are extremely rare; a notable exception, an ivory group of two women and a child from Mycenae, may represent two goddesses and a divine child. Some children were clearly highly valued, notably the two buried in one of the Mycenae shaft graves, each wrapped in a suit of thin sheet gold (fig. 24). Children's bones, being so small and

87. Terracotta of a woman holding a baby.

88. Miniature vases and feeding bottles such as these were often found in the tombs of children.

fragile, tend not to survive in the tomb, so little trace is left of them. On some painted *larnakes* from Tanagra, though, we see the bodies of small children being treated with loving care and being greatly mourned. On one of them, for instance, the scene shows two women bending over and gently laying the body of a small child into a coffin.

SCRIBES

Apart from the king and the warrior aristocracy, the tablets also indicate whole groups of people who held important positions in the Mycenaean courts, many of whom have left little trace of themselves in the archaeological record. The very existence of the tablets, of course, shows that many scribes were at work – those who wrote the signs and ideograms of Linear B; a study has been undertaken of the handwriting on the various tablets and many different hands have been identified. Although it's possible that Linear B was written almost exclusively by professional scribes who were trained for the purpose, it is likely that literacy was more widespread than that. Officials able to read and write were perhaps put in charge of various areas of production or of particular palace storerooms. The same hand, for instance, has been identified as having written the tablets concerned with wool, cloth and women workers at Knossos, probably the palace official in charge of textile production there. Scribal hands have also been recognised amongst those regulating the perfumed oil industry at Pylos, some of whom apparently had responsibility for goods in just one specific room of the palace, whilst another had written tablets found throughout different rooms as well as in the archive; perhaps he was the head of the administrative department with overall responsibility for the production of the oil. Personal touches amongst the tablets include the doodled sketches sometimes found on them and spelling mistakes and missed-out signs.

LOCAL ADMINISTRATION

Outside the confines of the palace and the court there were major landholders who seem to have acted as local administrators on behalf of the palace. In the case of Pylos, the territory controlled by the palace was divided into sixteen districts, each ruled by a governor, or mayor, the *koreter* (*ko-re- te*), and his deputy the *prokoreter* (*po-ro-ko-re-te*). The *prokoreter* has a subsidiary title of 'key-bearer', a term which is found elsewhere in the tablets associated with a woman who has been identified as a priestess. The governor and his deputy were probably at the head of a group called the *telestai* (*te-re-ta*) – high-ranking men listed in large numbers and thought to be independent landowners or yeomen living in areas controlled by the palace.

LIVES OF THE ORDINARY MEN AND WOMEN

Somewhere in-between the extremes of court official and slave there was a whole gamut of professions. Those who had land, even as sub-tenants, were probably the top level of the ordinary people of the kingdom. The term *damos* found in the tablets corresponds to the later Greek word *demos,* which means 'the people'. At Sphagianes in the Pylian kingdom, the *damos* holds communal land and is perhaps meant to mean the community in some way. The sub-tenants of plots of land listed at Sphagianes also include a few royal craftsmen who presumably had a higher status than most of their fellows. Also listed are people called 'servants of the deity', perhaps a reference to those concerned in some way with the official cult of the palace.

The basis of the Mycenaean kingdom was pastoral, and agricultural prosperity lay at its heart. On a basic agricultural level, the kingdom must have relied on the land it controlled for the growing of staple crops, for animal husbandry for meat, hides and wool and the growing of flax for making cloth. In the Linear B tablets we find meticulous regulation of all of these: women are listed as working flax, for instance, and men are shepherds, cowherds and goatherds.

CRAFT-WORKERS

The objects found in Mycenaean palaces, settlements and tombs show clearly just how wide a range of skills were held by the craft-workers in Mycenaean society.[5] Many different trades are also listed in the Linear B tablets, indicating a quite remarkable level of craft specialization, ranging from fundamentally important craft-workers like masons and bronzesmiths to those who provided luxuries for the palace elite, such as a 'maker of blue glass paste'. Some may have worked independently and sold their goods to the palaces, but those working in some of the industries, notably bronze-working (which used expensive raw materials, particularly tin) and the production of high-status commodities such as textiles and perfumed oils, did so under the close control and supervision of the palace élites.

The working of bronze (copper alloyed with tin) was vital to the Mycenaeans. Although there was iron ore in Greece, the technology to work it was not yet known and so the principal metal for tools, weapons and metal vessels was bronze. The Linear B tablets from Pylos give us an insight into the way the bronze industry there was organized. It has been calculated that in the area controlled by the palace there were about 400 smiths at work. The palace acquired the necessary raw materials and allotted them to craftsmen. Interestingly, bronze itself was distributed, as opposed to the copper and tin needed to make it. This was certainly the case at Nichoria (probably to be identified as the site called *ti-mi-to-a-ke-e* on the tablets), where we know from the archive that palace bronzesmiths were working. A bronze-smithy excavated there from the second half of the thirteenth century shows that they were reworking bronze rather than alloying copper and tin to make bronze. Some of the smiths listed in the tablets were not given any metal at all, and others were only given small quantities, indicating that there may have been a shortage of bronze in the last years of the palace.

Some tablets say what is to happen to the bronze that is being distributed – such as at Pylos where some metal is allocated for the making of arrowheads and spearheads – but in general our picture of what the bronzesmiths made with their raw materials is determined by what has survived in tombs: weapons and armour, vessels (cups, jugs, buckets, ladles, bowls), razors, tweezers, pins, mirrors, fibulae and tools like sickles, knives, axes and chisels. Important items like the large bronze tripod cauldrons we see being carried on the Pylos hunt fresco painting (fig. 89) are listed carefully on the tablets, including the damaged ones.

The palace also provided the ingredients needed for perfuming olive oil. A series of tablets from the archive room at Pylos gives us some idea of how the perfumed oils were made and others, many of them found in the oil store behind the Pylos megaron, meticulously

89. Large hunting dogs on leashes accompany men carrying cauldrons on a hunt fresco from Pylos.

record the finished oils, describing them with the ideogram for oil plus an adjective. From these we know that the oils might be scented – with flowers like roses, or herbs such as sage – or dyed, for instance with henna. These perfumed oils might be given as high-value gifts or as offerings to a deity. They were also traded abroad; although this is not mentioned in the tablets, we see the tangible remains in the stirrup-jars that once contained them traded around the Mediterranean.

Another crucial element in the economy of a Mycenaean kingdom was the textile industry. References to it are found on tablets from Mycenae, Thebes, Pylos and Knossos. At Pylos the industry was very centralized, with specific people located within the kingdom and at Pylos itself in control of it. The Mycenae and Thebes tablets record wool that has been collected and is to be redistributed for further work. They were found in buildings that may well have been storerooms for wool belonging to the palaces. The Linear B tablets which show the palace controlling textile production are not concerned with this domestic production or with ordinary cloth, but with the production of special kinds of textiles made from both wool and linen for the court and for the family of the king, and some may have been made for export. Domestic spinning and weaving of wool into cloth must have been a common activity all over the Mycenaean world, presumably carried out by women in the home for their own families.

Spinners, carders and weavers are listed and also more specific terms, which we are not able to recognize, for more specialist processes or types of material. Linen, for instance, was used for clothing and battle tunics, and could also have been used for the sails of ships. Thus the tablets reveal a complex industry for the making of fine textiles, and the finished products of this industry are seen worn by the men and women depicted in fresco paintings.

The Knossos tablets list large numbers of women working in the textile industry in several main towns within the area controlled by the palace. Some groups were making the cloth itself and others decorative attachments for it. Female workers are also recorded for the kingdom of Pylos, and rations of food are issued to them. The textile workers are listed with their children, but no husbands, and they appear to have had a very humble status. It is often difficult to establish from the tablets whether they were just low-born or in fact were slaves.

The building of the Mycenaean palaces and fortress walls would have demanded not simply stonemasons and a large work-force to move massive blocks of stone, but also many other kinds of specialized craftsmen. Highly skilled engineers, for example, would have been needed to overcome various problems presented by the construction of the fortifications, such as the building of the retaining wall to encompass Grave Circle A within the walls of Mycenae. Other major projects will have included tunnelling and construction of underground passages to secure water supplies at Mycenae, Tiryns and Athens, the building of roads and bridges linking areas of the kingdoms, the complex drainage system of Lake Kopais and the diverting of rivers at Tiryns and Pylos.

Coarse-ware pottery, such as cooking vessels, could have been made locally by relatively unskilled people, but the best products of fine-ware, both vases and figurines, would have required the skills of specialist craftsmen, reaching as they did an extremely high standard of production and artistry; they are listed along with goldsmiths, bowyers and saddlers on one Pylos tablet, while another mentions a royal potter, presumably making particularly fine items for the king. Ideograms for the various shapes of vases – some of clay, others in precious metals – are found on the tablets.

Fine wares from the fourteenth and thirteenth centuries demonstrate the standardization of shape and decoration that was to characterize the period of the Mycenaean *koine*, a term which refers to a time when a very uniform culture was spread across the Mycenaean world in the palace era. Amongst the most elegant products were the *kylikes*, long-stemmed drinking goblets. Some plain unpainted vases, usually *kylikes* and bowls, have patches of black encrustation on them, indicating that they were once coated in molten tin to form cheaper imitations of such vessels in silver.

Craft-workers specializing in the two-dimensional arts were clearly also at work in the palaces, the best of them employed in painting the walls and floors of palace buildings with brightly coloured frescoes. Less skilled painters decorated the class of vases known as 'Pictorial Style', often appearing to draw their inspiration from contemporary frescoes. These vases, painted with lively scenes, were made in the Argolid, probably principally for the overseas market, as so many of them have been found abroad, especially on the island of Cyprus. Many of these are decorated with scenes of people riding in chariots, but the artists also painted human figures, birds and animals that were familiar to them (for instance egrets, bulls and deer), and mythical beasts (such as griffins and sphinxes).

Other metals were also worked by Mycenaean craftsmen. The Mycenaeans from their earliest days showed a great fondness for gold and it continued to be their preferred precious metal in the palace era. Gold is identified on the Linear B tablets either by its ideogram or by the word *khrusos*. Vessels and elements of very fine furniture are listed on the tablets as being made of gold and a tablet from Pylos mentions goldsmiths amongst other tradesmen. Gold items found in contemporary tombs include vessels, jewellery and plaques from ornamental boxes, which were probably made of wood. Some silver items are also found on the tablets: the wheels of what must be a particularly splendid chariot are bound with silver instead of the usual bronze. Silver is not at all common on the tablets, though, unless its ideogram has not yet been recognized. Lead, like silver, was mined at Laurion and was used for making small figurines and other small cast objects.

Skilled ivory-carvers must have been working in the palace workshops to produce the exquisitely made objects of elephant and hippopotamus ivory that have been found. Ivory inlays were used to decorate furniture and boxes and chests listed in the tablets and ivory was carved to make toilet items, such as cosmetic boxes, combs, spatulas, small spoons, hairpins and needles – items often found in high-ranking women's graves. Also some jewellery was carved from ivory, from small pendants to more splendid items like the three ivory crowns found in the ruins of the Treasury at Thebes. Stone-carvers used fine stones to make decorative relief panels for the walls of palaces and façades of tombs and also vessels, such as *pyxides* (boxes) of alabaster. Their most delicate art, though, was the carving of exquisitely detailed scenes on semi-precious seal-stones.

Workshops where craftsmen made such products from these precious materials have been identified at the palaces, within which we find scraps of raw materials and sometimes tablets and sealings to indi-

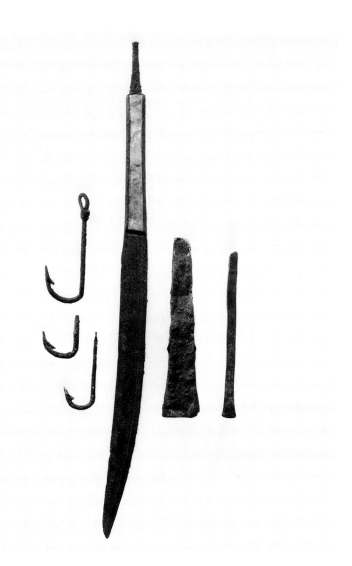

90. Personal objects that the deceased used during their lifetime were placed with them in the grave: fish hooks, bronze knife with an ivory handle, chisel and awl from tombs at Ialysos, Rhodes.

cate what was being made there. Fine local and imported raw materials were being used there to make luxuries for the palace élite. At Mycenae, workshops found in the east wing of palace on the summit of the acropolis contain evidence for the working of gold, ivory and semi-precious stones – imported luxuries brought to Greece on trading routes from the East.

Some people's professions can be determined from the contents of their tombs, as Mycenaeans were often buried with the tools of their trade: chisels and other wood-working tools found in graves, for instance, probably indicate the burial there of a carpenter. A tomb at Perati on the coast of Attica contained a whole set of bronze fish hooks and the lead weights that once would have been attached to a fishing net, and so clearly was the resting-place of a fisherman. Similarly, a lyre made from a tortoise shell found in a tholos tomb at Menidhi must once have belonged to a bard, like the one who was painted on the wall of the megaron at Pylos, seated on a rock and playing his lyre. Another tomb, this time at Nauplion, contained a set of bronze surgical implements, dating to around 1450 BC. The instruments included drills, scalpels, tweezers and large forceps. Doctors and surgeons have not been identified amongst the professions listed on the tablets, but this must be the burial of one. Studies of Mycenaean skeletal remains certainly show that the Mycenaeans practised trepanation and successfully set badly broken bones – procedures requiring medical expertise.

Doctors and bards would have been few in number, of course, and at the opposite end of the scale we have the very large numbers of men who are listed simply in the Pylos tablets as the 800 who were sent to watch the coast and the 500–600 men who worked as rowers in the fleet.

SLAVES

The tablets tell us that the royal officials had large numbers of dependants and slaves, both men and women. We can see from the tablets that there was widespread slavery in Mycenaean Greece, at least in those areas controlled by the palace at Pylos, and, by inference, at other such centres. The Linear B word for slave was *do-we-ro/ra*, giving us the word *dowelos*, which in Classical Greek was *doulos*, slave. Men, women and children are listed as slaves on the tablets, though there are far fewer male than female slaves. Some of them have ethnic adjectives attached to their names, indicating their origins. They come from such areas as Asia Minor; women from Miletos, Knidos and from the island of Lemnos. Some of these foreign slaves may have been acquired on raids abroad as several of the women are said to be *ra-wi-ja-ja,* meaning captives. A number of the women slaves were employed as flax-workers, grinders of corn and bath attendants; amongst the male slaves are those listed as belonging to bronzesmiths, so they may well have been skilled. The actual status of some groups of slaves is difficult to determine: the term 'slave of the god', for example, may either refer to a slave belonging to the god or be an honorary title for one who serves the deity.

9

Mycenaean Religion

The tangible traces of Mycenaean worship and religious belief that we find in the archaeological record are tantalizingly fragmentary, but they do give us some of the most evocative artefacts and wall paintings to have survived from Mycenaean Greece. What we find in the ground are not the beliefs themselves, of course, but rather what has been left behind as a consequence of those beliefs. This may include images of deities and their worshippers, cult buildings and other places of worship, and objects used in the rituals involved, such as altars and *rhyta* (ritual sprinkling vessels). Having written records ought to fill out this picture, but Linear B tablets are not inscribed with anything like myths or religious writing. They do, however, give us names of deities, places where they were worshipped and the kinds of offerings made to them. From these three main sources of evidence (archaeological excavations of cult areas and sanctuaries, representations in art and the written texts on Linear B tablets) we will recreate what we can of Mycenaean religion.[1]

Early studies of religion in the Bronze Age Aegean spoke of Minoan–Mycenaean religion, conflating the two into one whole. This is because the religious iconography of the Mycenaeans, particularly in the Shaft Grave Era (1600–1450 BC), looks very Minoan in character, focusing as it does on a predominant goddess or goddesses. Furthermore, the only shrine of the Shaft Grave Era excavated so far on the Greek mainland, that of Apollo Maleatas at Epidauros, has an open-air altar, conical cups and bronze double-axes, all of which have clear affinities with the ritual observances of the Minoans. This was a time of heavy borrowing, though, of Minoan iconography in general by the Mycenaeans, and it may well be that they were adopting Minoan symbolism rather than Minoan beliefs. Both archaeology and Linear B tablets have clearly demonstrated that Mycenaean religion in fact had a clearly recognizable character of its own.

SHRINES OF THE MYCENAEANS

The places where the Mycenaeans worshipped their gods ranged from formal areas set aside within the palaces to special religious centres and

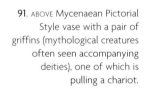

91. ABOVE Mycenaean Pictorial Style vase with a pair of griffins (mythological creatures often seen accompanying deities), one of which is pulling a chariot.

92. RIGHT A winged sphinx wearing a *polos* (headdress); a detail from a Cypriot Rude Style *krater* (bowl) made in imitation of Mycenaean Pictorial Style vases.

simple open-air shrines.[2] Some sites may have been for official or urban religion and others for popular or rural worship; ostentatious rituals as opposed to day-to-day observances. Few open-air shrines have been found, perhaps because they left little to mark where they had been, though that of Apollo Maleatas near Epidauros continued in use in subsequent centuries, and two others of later date have been found near Tiryns.

The tangible remains of cult centres in the Mycenaean world have been excavated in some of the palaces, for instance at Mycenae and Tiryns, and in urban centres at non-palatial sites, notably at Methana, Phylakopi on Melos and Ayia Irini on Kea. They are identified as such by the frescoes that decorated their walls, by the paraphernalia of cult found in them and by figurines, some of them worshippers, others perhaps representing the deities themselves. Linear B tablets also reveal that there were important religious centres outside the palaces, to which offerings were sent from the palace élites. Who then were the deities worshipped by the Mycenaeans and what forms did this worship take?

The Cult Centre at Mycenae
Perhaps our best chance of beginning to answer such a question comes from a study of the Cult Centre at the palace of Mycenae, which is

93. Mycenaean silver bowl, thirteenth century BC, from Enkomi, Cyprus.

94. ABOVE Mycenaean seal-stones. Clockwise from top left: carnelian lentoid seal with three deer, one grazing; rock-crystal lentoid seal with two prancing goats; lapis lazuli cushion-shaped seal in a gold mount engraved with a lion and a tree; red agate lentoid seal with a bull grazing; glass intaglio with a lion; and green jasper lentoid seal with a lion attacking a goat.

95. RIGHT Cup of the late fourteenth century BC decorated with birds, fish and 'horns of consecration' (stylized bulls' horns), the latter a motif found often in Minoan religious contexts.

96. ABOVE Two clay bull-head *rhyta* (ritual sprinkling vessels), thirteenth century BC, the one on the left from Karpathos and the one on the right from Enkomi.

97. RIGHT Terracotta bulls and a trick vase (which appears empty until poured) with a bull-head spout, thirteenth century BC.

98. ABOVE Terracotta goddess seated on a throne with her legs curled up and a group of three women performing a sacred dance, thirteenth century BC.

99. Pottery *kalathos* (bowl) with three female figures standing on its rim, twelfth century BC.

built on land within the walls of the fortified acropolis, on terraces on the lower slopes close to the wall. It consists of five building complexes, dating from the late fourteenth to mid-thirteenth centuries, perhaps built successively, with Shrine Gamma appearing to be the earliest. Earthquake damage in the middle of the thirteenth century led to extensive rebuilding of the complex and the shrine as it is today dates mainly to the second half of the thirteenth century, though some of the sacred objects and figurines found in it are of the early fourteenth century. Presumably highly prized items had been moved from an earlier sacred area elsewhere and incorporated into the rituals taking place within the new Cult Centre.

From the Cult Centre at Mycenae comes the most clearly identifiable of all Mycenaean deities – a warrior goddess (fig. 104). Found in the debris between Tsountas' House and the South-west Building were the remains of a fresco executed in miniature against a blue ground. One fragment preserves an exquisite depiction of the upper part of a white-skinned figure, her warlike nature indicated by the ornate boar's-tusk helmet she wears on her head. She carries in her arms a small winged griffin, which turns its head back to look at her face. Griffins were imaginary creatures, winged and with the head of an eagle and the body of a lion, and are often found accompanying a deity in both Minoan and Mycenaean art. Near to her was found another fragment, also in miniature and against the same blue ground, depicting three donkey-headed daemons carrying a long pole or pulling a

100. RIGHT Fragment of a Mycenaean Pictorial Style vase showing a pair of men boxing, a ritual sport known to us from Minoan iconography.

101. OPPOSITE Mycenaean side-spouted sieve-jug of the thirteenth century BC, decorated with a man grasping the horns of a bull, reminiscent of the Minoan ritual sport of bull-leaping.

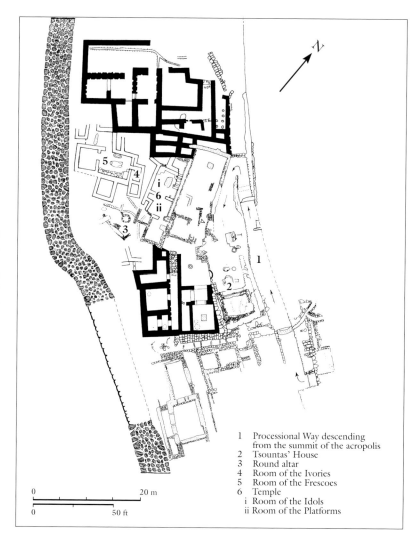

102. Plan of the Cult Centre at Mycenae.

103. OPPOSITE Just under life-size painted plaster head, probably of a goddess, from Mycenae.

0	20 m
0	50 ft

1 Processional Way descending from the summit of the acropolis
2 Tsountas' House
3 Round altar
4 Room of the Ivories
5 Room of the Frescoes
6 Temple
i Room of the Idols
ii Room of the Platforms

rope on their shoulders (fig. 105). Such daemons are also seen making offerings to a seated goddess on a large gold signet ring discovered in a hoard at Tiryns. The daemon derives ultimately from the Egyptian hippopotamus goddess Taweret (*Ta-urt*), whose iconography was adopted by the Minoans and thence transmitted to the Mycenaeans. The warrior goddess and the daemons are probably both surviving fragments from the same scene. Perhaps the same warrior goddess is painted on a stucco tablet from Tsountas' House: two women, their arms held forwards in a gesture of adoration, flank a goddess, whose entire body – except her arms, head and possibly her feet – is covered by a figure-of-eight shield. A frieze of large figure-of-eight shields used as a decorative motif was also painted on the walls of the South-west Building.

104. Warrior Goddess, wearing a boar's-tusk helmet and carrying a small griffin, painted on a wall of the Cult Centre at Mycenae.

Within the Cult Centre there are several distinct areas, defined as such both by their architecture and by the cult images and ritual paraphernalia found in them. They may have been set apart for the worship of different deities, though they have elements in common. The two areas which give us the greatest insight into the deities worshipped there by the people of Mycenae are the complexes of the Room of the Frescoes and the place known as the 'Temple'. The first of these two complexes was reached via an anteroom, which led into the Room of the Frescoes, to one side of which was a storeroom and to the other the Room of the Ivories. The Room of the Frescoes was the main chamber of the complex, decorated with frescoes as its name implies, and lying on an east-west axis. A large oval hearth lay in the centre of the room, to the north of which was a terracotta *larnax* or bathtub, perhaps for some form of bathing ritual. Along the east wall was a stuccoed bench, with ash in some indentations at one end, which probably was used as an altar. It was decorated in fresco technique with 'horns of consecration' (stylized bulls' horns); the only really Minoan feature of the entire Mycenae Cult Centre. Lying on the floor in front of the altar was found an exceptionally fine male head carved in ivory.

105. Donkey-headed daemons, pulling or carrying a rope, on a fresco from the Cult Centre at Mycenae.

The wall behind the altar was decorated with a fresco: a woman and an animal are partially preserved (possibly a goddess with a griffin) and in the register above them are two robed female figures (perhaps again warrior goddesses), one carrying a large sword and the other a staff, whilst between them two small male figures (maybe worshippers) appear to float in the air. The adjacent Room of the Ivories, part of this complex, was L-shaped. At its southern end was a platform on which stood a small decorated female figurine (perhaps a goddess) with ornaments in front of her. These included a pile of glass beads, which were presumably the remains of a necklace given as an offering. Other areas of the room appear to have been used for storage; the presence there of significant quantities of ivory has given the room its name.

From the area of the Cult Centre that included the Room of the Platforms and the Room of the Idols (sometimes called the Temple of

106. Detail from the wall painting of goddesses from the Room of the Frescoes in the Cult Centre at Mycenae.

107. Fresco of a woman known as the 'Lady Of Mycenae' carrying a necklace from the Cult Centre at Mycenae.

Mycenae) comes evidence that although a warrior goddess was central to ritual at the palace, other deities may well have been worshipped there too. In these two rooms stood a number of wheel-made terracotta figurines of exceptional size, forbidding expression and marked individuality, perhaps to be interpreted as depictions of deities rather than simply of worshippers. The main chamber, approached via a vestibule, is known as the Room of the Platforms because it contained several low platforms built at different heights. On the highest of these stood the most formidable of the terracotta figurines, with a small table of offerings in front of her. To the right, a staircase led up to the Room of the Idols, where more of the terracotta figures were found, together with tables of offering, terracotta snakes and a few clay vases; other figures were also found in an alcove.

In total, nineteen large figures were found (*c.*60 cm [some 2 ft] tall), along with four smaller ones (about half the height), decorated and more benevolent in appearance, and a few terracotta figurines of more usual type, together with seventeen coiled snakes. The large-scale figurines were all different from each other: some were recognizably female with breasts and tresses of hair; while others were bald and had no breasts, perhaps to be interpreted as males. They did not all belong to the same era, with some being of the early fourteenth century and others of the thirteenth, contemporary with the building. Some of the figures have upraised arms and others were apparently holding objects, perhaps cult objects, the handles of some of which remain. One large figure of indeterminate gender is still holding a hammer-axe. These attributes may have been signifiers by which the specific deities were recognized. We cannot be so specific as to link any of them with the named deities in Linear B, but they at least show that the Mycenaeans did have a conception of a multiplicity of deities.

The South-west Building, otherwise known as 'The House of the High Priest', may also have formed part of the Mycenae Cult Centre. From this building comes an important procession fresco of women, with most standing but at least two sitting. The figures on this fresco include the so-called 'Lady of Mycenae': a life-size woman, shown with her body turned to the front and her face in profile. She is wearing a short-sleeved yellow bodice and a blue blouse. She wears one necklace and holds another in her hand. She may be either a goddess who has just been given the necklace as an offering, or is perhaps a worshipper, making a gift (as we saw in the gift of a glass bead necklace on an altar in the Room of the Ivories). On another wall in the same room were a seated figure and an interesting fragment showing a pair of hands holding a small female figure, which may represent the offering of a child to the goddess, or the gift of a votive figurine.

The overwhelming impression gained from the Mycenae Cult Centre is that the Mycenaeans mainly worshipped female deities. However, some of the large terracottas from the 'Temple' might well be male, and the ivory head from the Room of the Frescoes could be that of a male deity. Furthermore, fragmentary male figurines from Tiryns and Athens and more complete examples from Phylakopi on Melos show that male deities were also worshipped, a suggestion born out by the evidence of Linear B, which reveals for us a world in which the Mycenaeans were clearly worshipping a number of both male and female deities.

Tiryns

From nearby Tiryns comes further evidence for cult practice in the Mycenaean palaces. Pockets of cult activity from the second half of the thirteenth century have been excavated on the upper and lower citadel, but the best-preserved remains of ritual activity are those of the post-palatial, twelfth-century phase of the settlement, found within the walls of the lower citadel. These consist of a sequence of freestanding shrines associated with mainly female figurines with upraised arms and figures of animals. However, a phallus, broken off from what must have been a large male clay figure, has also been found here, and represents the remains of one of only two such figurines known from the mainland; the other came from the acropolis at Athens. The only other male deities are smiting gods (bronze figures of deities of a type known from Cyprus and Syro-Palestine) found at Mycenae and Tiryns, which are clearly imported from the East.

Ayios Konstantinos on Methana

From the site of Ayios Konstantinos, on the volcanic peninsula of Methana in the Saronic Gulf comes further evidence for the possible worship of a male deity. A three-chamber shrine has been excavated here, with pottery (including tripods, *rhyta* and *kylikes*) dating to the fourteenth and thirteenth centuries. In the main room were found a stepped stone bench, a platform and a hearth, together with pottery vessels associated with libation rituals (a *kylix*, cup and dipper) in one corner. Associated with the bench were around one hundred and fifty clay figurines, some of which were of rare types, such as helmeted figures riding horses and people driving or riding oxen. It might be reasonable to suppose that these are male, given their activities; only one female figurine of *psi* type (named after its similarity in shape to the letter of the Greek alphabet) has been found.

Phylakopi on Melos

Identifiably male figurines are known on Crete in thirteenth-century contexts at Khania and the Unexplored Mansion at Knossos, and in one of the twelfth century at Ayia Triadha. The best evidence though for worship of a male god in the Aegean comes from the shrine excavated at Phylakopi on Melos, dating to the fourteenth and thirteenth centuries, at a time when the island was either under Mycenaean control or had at least a strongly Mycenaean character. It presents us with a very different picture to that of the Mycenaean palace cult centres and, as such, amply demonstrates the lack of uniformity of cult in the Mycenaean world. There were two shrines: the East Shrine and the larger West Shrine. The West Shrine was constructed first (around 1360 BC), with a second phase dating to the building of the defensive wall at the site; the East Shrine was then added around 1270 BC. In front of the doorway of the West Shrine stood a large rounded stone or *baetyl* – a sacred stone like those seen in cult scenes depicted in Aegean iconography, for instance on a gold ring found in Sellopoulo Tomb 4 on Crete.

Worship of both gods and goddesses in this shrine was clearly indicated, and they seem to have been worshipped at different altars according to their gender. In the north-west corner of the West Shrine was an altar from which had toppled a female *psi* figurine and a series of extraordinary terracotta figurines clearly defined as male by their genitals. It therefore appears that this altar was dedicated to the worship of one or more male deities. In the south-west corner stood another altar, again with a *psi* figurine but this time accompanied by a second female figure, perhaps for the worship of female deities. To the west of the West Shrine, in a small room, were found yet more figurines, including the headless body of a large female figurine known as the Lady of Phylakopi, her head subsequently found nearby, together with parts of two other figures. In a niche in the east wall were found four terracotta wheel-made bulls and a grotesque head. Outside the area of the two shrines, but clearly belonging with what was found within them, was a bronze figure of a smiting god. Around 1120 BC the whole shrine complex collapsed, suffering severe damage, but it was repaired and re-used, and the earlier cult images continued to be worshipped until it finally went out of use around 1090 BC.

Ayia Irini on Kea

Another island shrine, even earlier in date, was found at Ayia Irini on the island of Kea, dating from *c.*1500 BC. The finds from this shrine, very distinct in character, include several very large, almost life-size, terracotta female figurines.

The iconography of both Minoan religion and Mycenaean religion appears overwhelmingly to point to the pre-eminence of the worship of a goddess. The complex of shrines and altars at the Mycenae Cult Centre seem to imply pluralism, with a multiplicity of deities being worshipped, but again the impression gained is of goddesses as opposed to gods. Only at Phylakopi, and perhaps at Methana, do we at last have in the archaeological record a clear reflection of what we see on the Linear B tablets – namely that the Mycenaeans worshipped both male and female deities.

RELIGION AND LINEAR B

Linear B tablets give us no religious texts, no myths and no hymns to deities. What they do give us is a picture of the palace regulating the official religion of the kingdom, thus providing three main classes of information: the names of gods and goddesses, the offerings made to them and sometimes the names of religious centres.[3]

The texts inscribed on the Linear B tablets confirm what has tentatively begun to emerge from the archaeological record. They show us that the Mycenaeans were already worshipping a whole pantheon of deities, both male and female, as we can see that the Greeks did from the eighth century onwards, when we again have written records. The multiplicity of deities seen in the eighth-century works of Homer and Hesiod reflects a system of belief that goes back to the Bronze Age. Some of the gods and goddesses from the eighth century are already identifiable by name in the Linear B tablets, though there is no guarantee, of course, that their nature or function remained the same.

Which gods and goddesses then can we see as far back as the Bronze Age? If we search the tablets for early forms of the names of the twelve Olympian deities of Classical Greece (Zeus, Hera, Poseidon, Athena, Apollo, Artemis, Hermes, Demeter, Hephaistos, Aphrodite, Ares and Dionysos) we find that many of them are recognizable. Unfortunately, Linear B does not indicate in any way that a named individual is a deity. Only names on the tablets that appear in a clearly religious context can be definitely identified as deities, both familiar and unfamiliar.

One name for a goddess (or goddesses), who appears relatively frequently on tablets from both Pylos and Knossos, is Potnia. Occasionally it appears as a name on its own, but it is usually qualified by epithets, and it is hard to tell whether these references refer to different goddesses or to different aspects of the same goddess. On one tablet from Knossos she has the title *a-ta-na po-ti-ni-ja* (Athana Potnia) which means 'Mistress Athena', a term for the goddess Athena known to us from Homeric epic. Another tablet from the same palace refers to 'Potnia of the Labyrinth' and from Pylos we have a reference to 'Potnia of the Horses'. In Classical Greek, Demeter and Persephone were known as the Potniai, and it may be that the Mycenaean goddess Potnia was the name for an earth or mother goddess.

From the Knossos tablet which gave us the name Athana Potnia comes the names of three other deities who are familiar to us from later Greek written sources: *e-nu- wa-ri-jo* is Enualios, an alternative name for Ares, god of war; *pa-ja-wo* resembles the Homeric Paieon, later Paian, an alternative name for Apollo; and *po-se-da (o)*, Poseidaon. Thus within these two brief lines on one tablet we have the early forms of names of Athena, Ares, Apollo and Poseidon. It is clear from tablets from the palace of Pylos that Poseidon was the pre-eminent deity worshipped there. Homer may retain a memory of this in his mention of a festival to Poseidon at Pylos (*Odyssey*, iii, 43).

The god Dionysos has also been tentatively identified on the tablets. His name, in the form Diwonusos, appears twice at Pylos, but both tablets are too fragmentary to make it certain the name is referring to a god. Until his name was found on the tablets it was believed that his worship only began in Greece after the end of the Dark Age. Similarly the name Haphaistios appears at Knossos, perhaps an indication that the smith-god Hephaistos was already worshipped in Mycenaean times. Another tablet from Pylos bore the names Zeus, Hera and Hermes. Female names derived from the names of Zeus and Poseidon are also listed on the tablets. Other deities, who have a minor role in later

Greek literature but were not amongst the Olympians, are also found, such as Iphimedeia, who is known from Homer's *Odyssey* to have had two sons by the god Poseidon.

Although the names of some deities are found on tablets from the mainland and from Crete, others are found only on those from Knossos and probably record deities specific to the island. Diktaian Zeus (named after the Dikte Mountain on Crete) and Eilytheia (the Cretan goddess of childbirth) appear, as one might expect, only on the tablets from Knossos. Homer, in the *Odyssey*, talks of the cave of Eilytheia at Amnisos, and the cave has been found and excavated. The term 'all the gods' again appears only at Knossos and may perhaps be a reference to a group of Minoan deities. Similarly at Knossos, but not Pylos, we have the term 'Priestess of the Winds'. Several names on the Knossos tablets have not been identified and this may be because they are Minoan deities, notably the goddess *pi-pi-tu-na*, whose name has the same non-Greek ending as that of the more familiar Cretan goddess Dictynna. It was probably expedient for the new Mycenaean rulers of the palace of Knossos to incorporate worship of the established Minoan deities as well as introducing their own from the mainland.

The Linear B texts provide no real clues as to the nature of the deities listed, and we cannot assume that simply because they have the same name as one of the Olympians they already had the same character in Mycenaean times. That one of the Mycenaean deities was a god of healing is perhaps indicated by a Hittite divination text from the capital Hattusa, dating to *c.*1350–320 BC. It reports that King Mursili was cured with the help of a cult statuette of the god of Ahhijawa, a term believed to be the Hittite name for Mycenaean Greece. It may perhaps have been Paion, identified by name on the tablets and known from the time of Homer as a god of healing, who cured the Hittite king.

OFFERINGS AND CULT PRACTICE

The tablets listing named deities were often written by palace officials in order to record the offerings that were to be made to those deities, sometimes at a named place of worship outside the confines of the palace. It is therefore clear that official rituals of the Mycenaean élites were not only performed within cult centres in palaces, but also at designated sacred places elsewhere. Offerings, for instance, were sent from the palace at Knossos to deities some distance away at Amnisos. Amnisos was clearly an important and prestigious religious centre for the worship of the goddess Eilytheia as well as other deities.

A wide variety of goods were considered suitable offerings for the gods and goddesses of the Mycenaeans: these include gold vessels, wool, perfumed oil, barley, figs, flour, wine, olive oil and honey. Processions of people (usually women) painted on the walls of the palaces may well be a pictorial expression of such gift offering. The women are

108. Large copper pitcher (part of a drinking set) from a tomb.

usually wearing Minoan-style dress of flounced skirts and a tightly fitting bodice, exposing bare breasts and carrying offerings. On the walls of the Kadmeia at Thebes they carry such gifts as a bunch of roses, a stone vase and a box. A similar fragmentary scene from Tiryns preserves parts of at least eight women carrying such objects as a *pyxis* (a small lidded container) and a terracotta figurine. From Mycenae perhaps as many as five such processional frescoes are known but they are very fragmentary. Uniquely for a mainland palace, the procession frescoes from Pylos have men taking part in the procession: the most complete is that of male and female figures from the walls of the vestibule of the megaron. The procession frescoes from the palaces and the evidence for cult activity within the megaron itself, particularly at Pylos which has libation channels in the floor and a possible ritual banquet painted on the wall near the throne, connects the *wanax* (king) himself with such activities.

Animals such as cows, pigs, goats, sheep and wild boar were also offered to the Mycenaean deities and were presumably intended to be sacrificed. Such a sacrifice is depicted on one side of the Ayia Triadha sarcophagus, dating to the period of Mycenaean rule on Crete. It shows a bull lying trussed on an altar and the blood pouring from his gashed throat being collected in a vessel. Deposits of ash and animal bone found at shrines like Phylakopi, Asine and Apollo Maleatas at Epidauros are the tangible remains of sacrifices. Such rituals may have been accompanied by ritual feasting and drinking in honour of the gods. A study of the vessels found in the Room of the Frescoes at the Mycenae Cult Centre has revealed that they contained the residues of meals which, given the context, were presumably ritual feasts or offerings to a deity: one large tripod cooking pot had once contained a meal of meat and lentils cooked in olive oil, while another had been used to cook fish in olive oil and wine. Such feasts are also seen in the Linear B tablets as taking place in honour of the *wanax*. These may be simply state banquets, but they could also reflect an aspect of the *wanax* as divine, much as the pharaoh of the Egyptians was both secular ruler and deity. A fresco from the wall of the megaron at Pylos, which incorporates a bard seated on a rock, men sitting engaged in a drinking ritual and the trussed figure of a bull, presumably reflects ritual feasting.

That the gods and goddesses of the Mycenaeans should have received animal sacrifice in their honour is not controversial; that they may also have received human sacrifice certainly is. Indications that this may indeed be the case are to be found on a few of the Linear B tablets. A large tablet from Pylos seems to be listing offerings to be made at a religious festival that took place during the month of *po-ro-wi-ti-jo*. As part of the ceremony, offerings were made to deities at Pylos itself and at a place called *pa-ki-ja- ne*, apparently an important religious centre dedicated to Poseidon. The goddess Potnia and other named individuals, probably to be identified as deities, are each offered a man or woman and a gold vessel. It has been suggested that this refers to figurines, which we see held on the frescoes as offerings, but the language used shows that they were to be led rather than carried and should therefore be a real human not just a representation of one. It may be that the offering of a human being simply refers to the gift of a servant to the deity, or it may reflect a human sacrifice.

Classical Greek literature is littered with references to human sacrifice, and bones found in the doorways of some Mycenaean tombs have been thought to be sacrificial victims. Actual sacrifice of a human being to a deity (as opposed to being part of funerary ritual) would only leave traces in the archaeological record under exceptional circumstances, such as those which preserved the sacrifice of a youth on an altar that took place at Archanes-Anemospilia on Crete around 1700 BC, when an earthquake caused the roof to collapse in on the shrine as the act took place.

FUNERARY RITUAL AND THE AFTERLIFE

Rituals for the benefit of the living were accompanied in Mycenaean society by those for the dead, and a question we might reasonably try to ask of the archaeological record is whether the Mycenaeans believed in some form of life after death.[4] There is no doubt that they invested a great deal of wealth in funerary display. This was particularly evident in the Shaft Grave Era and continued to be the case throughout the later centuries of the Mycenaean period. At Mycenae itself the three latest and most elaborate of the great tholos tombs outside the citadel walls, namely the Tomb of Clytemnestra, the Tomb of the Genii and the Treasury of Atreus, all built during the latter half of the fourteenth century, reached great heights of architectural sophistication. The Treasury of Atreus, also known as the Tomb of Agamemnon, was a particularly fine monument, with a façade decorated with coloured marble, carved in relief. A pair of half-columns of green marble, carved with zigzags and spirals, flanked the doorway, and slabs of red and green marble with spirals and a semi-rosette frieze covered the relieving triangle over the lintel of the doorway. Two slabs of gypsum perhaps came from the small side chamber of this tomb: one carved with the head of a bull, the other with the forelegs of another bull.

Although the tholos tombs at Mycenae had been very thoroughly robbed, and we can only guess at their contents, those of some rich chamber tombs from the site, and indeed from elsewhere in the Mycenaean world, demonstrate that the Mycenaeans of the palatial era continued to bury rich grave goods with their dead. That such efforts should have been gone to in the building of monumental tombs and in the provision of rich grave offerings shows the importance of death and its associated rituals to the Mycenaeans. However, this emphasis on funerary display was quite possibly to impress the living rather than to provide comfort for the dead.

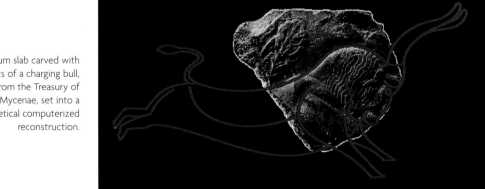

109. Gypsum slab carved with the foreparts of a charging bull, said to be from the Treasury of Atreus at Mycenae, set into a hypothetical computerized reconstruction.

110. Decorative carved-stone façade of the Treasury of Atreus (hypothetical computerized reconstruction).

Some items of a humble and personal nature, though, were also placed in tombs. They contributed little to the funerary display and must surely have been intended for the use of the dead: simple knives and tools, spindle-whorls, and toilet articles like ear-picks, mirrors and razors are commonly found. Small terracotta figurines were placed in graves, perhaps intended to care for or to accompany the dead in some way. Many were figures of women and came in three main forms, each named after letters of the Greek alphabet which they resemble – *phi*, *psi* and *tau*. Other terracottas placed in tombs were of animals, horse-drawn chariots and boats. Children were often buried with miniature vases and with feeding bottles (see fig. 88).

Animals such as dogs and horses have been found sacrificed at Mycenaean tombs. Horses were symbols of status, and those found in pairs perhaps pulled the funerary chariot or cart that carried the dead to the tomb. Sacrificed dogs, often buried in a doorway, were probably a favoured animal, placed there to guard their owner in death and perhaps to accompany them into the afterlife. The occasional finds of human bones at the doorways of tombs may represent a slave or servant burial, intended to serve their master or mistress in the afterlife.

Rituals that took place at funerals often leave their trace in the archaeological record, and we see smashed *kylikes* and animal bones in the dromos – evidence for ritual funerary feasting. A series of clay *larnakes* (coffins) from the Mycenaean chamber tomb cemetery at Tanagra in Boiotia (about 20 km [12 miles] from Thebes) throw further light on the funerary rituals of the Mycenaeans (see figs 114 and 115).[5] The cemetery was in use from the late fifteenth through to the mid-thirteenth century BC and the coffins were painted with brightly coloured depictions of funerals and their accompanying rituals. These

111. A pair of bronze 'razors' from a tomb at Ialysos on Rhodes.

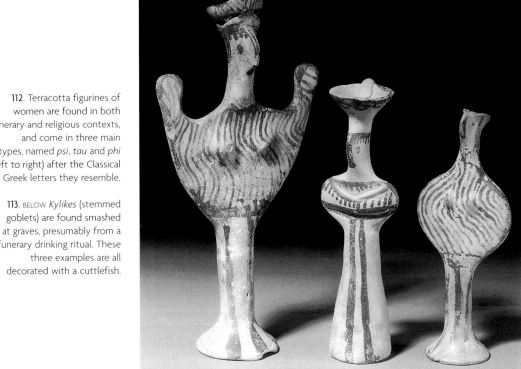

112. Terracotta figurines of women are found in both funerary and religious contexts, and come in three main types, named *psi*, *tau* and *phi* (left to right) after the Classical Greek letters they resemble.

113. BELOW *Kylikes* (stemmed goblets) are found smashed at graves, presumably from a funerary drinking ritual. These three examples are all decorated with a cuttlefish.

114. A row of women raise their hands to their heads in a gesture of mourning on the side of a *larnax* (coffin) from Tanagra, Boiotia.

115. BELOW One side of a terracotta *larnax* (coffin) decorated with scenes from a funeral, from Tanagra, Boiotia.

scenes are our most complete and detailed iconographical record of Mycenaean burial ritual. They include the *prothesis,* the lying in state of the dead, and the *ekphora,* the carrying of the body to the grave, as well as mourning and lamenting women. The pouring of libations and a possible animal sacrifice are also shown. Warriors fighting duels and racing each other in chariots are probably, given their context, taking part in funeral games. One *larnax* is decorated with many of these elements. The figures are drawn in red and black and appear in silhouette. On each short side is a row of mourning women set above a scene of the body of the deceased placed in *a larnax.* On one long side we have on the upper register a row of lamenting women, with their hands raised to their heads in a gesture of mourning, and on the lower, a chariot race and two warriors fighting a duel. The other long side carries on the upper register a man with a sword, surrounded by goats and striking the throat of one of them; below him is a rather disembodied rite of bull-leaping, in which the leaper appears to float above the back of the bull.

10

The Decline and Fall of the Mycenaeans

Shortly before 1200 BC there were signs that all was not well in the Mediterranean. Apparent interruptions to trading routes with the East, hints of problems of supply and demand from the Linear B tablets and the building of secure water supplies at several of the fortified palaces all point to a time of unrest and unease. The Mycenaeans clearly felt under threat and they were right – a terrible wave of destructions was to engulf their world and bring the Bronze Age to an end. But was it what they feared that actually destroyed them?

The peace and prosperity that had characterized the region for much of the previous two hundred years began to show signs of dislocation. The first signs had come with the localized destructions of some buildings that had taken place at some of the major sites just after the middle of the thirteenth century BC, but it was towards the end of this century that the picture became more widespread. Although some ships were still trading (as is indicated by the Cape Gelidonya and Pont Iria wrecks of around 1200 BC), the disruption to sea routes and thus to sea-borne trade is evident. The inhabitants of Cyprus – so important in contacts between east and west – appear to have experienced difficulties in importing the Mycenaean Pictorial Style vases they liked so much, and they began instead to make their own imitations (known as 'Rude' or 'Pastoral Style') in the last quarter of the thirteenth century.

Hints of problems with supply and demand in the Mediterranean are perhaps also to be seen in the Pylos Linear B tablets. The amounts of metals sent to various bronzesmiths in the kingdom appear to have been carefully rationed, which may indicate a shortage of such metals in Messenia in the final year of the life of the palace. It is, however, difficult to assess whether this was indeed the case as we have only the records from the one year and thus cannot compare the situation with that prevalent in other years; such rationing may have been standard practice. Furthermore, a limited supply of bronze was not necessarily the result of a disruption to sea trade: if the Mycenaeans were relying principally on copper from Laurion, shortages could have occurred through problems in the Argolid and Attica affecting exploitation of the mines there.

The clearest sign of threat to the established order, though, is the provision of secure water supplies to Mycenae, Tiryns and Athens. The rebuilding and expansion of fortress walls at Mycenae and Tiryns around the middle of the thirteenth century had greatly increased the fortified area and the power of both citadels. It is possible that these expansions were a visible flexing of their muscle – symbolic of great strength and owing more to inter-kingdom rivalries than to any threat from outside. However, additions to these fortifications towards the closing years of the century are entirely different in character and must surely have been in response to fears of prolonged attack or siege.

This final extension to the walls of Mycenae, around 1200 BC, added a small but highly significant and strategically important dog-leg to the north-east section of the citadel. Into the walls of the extension were built two galleries: the south gallery led to a small sally port giving access onto a low terrace with a view over the Khavos ravine; the north gallery led steeply down under the walls via a corbelled subterranean passageway to an underground cistern, ingeniously built in a

116. At the end of the thirteenth century BC a dog-leg was added to the citadel of Mycenae, with a sally port and a secure water supply.

natural fold of the bedrock and fed by clay pipes bringing water from natural springs. This construction assured a secure water supply to the fortress if attack or siege made access to springs outside the walls too dangerous.

At Tiryns similar precautions were taken at the same time. Towards the end of the thirteenth century the people of Tiryns doubled the size of the fortified area of the citadel, taking the lower hill to the north within its protective orbit. To the south, the extended wall was so wide that a whole series of storage rooms could be built within its thickness, together with galleries with corbelled roofs. To the east, an extra wall was built to strengthen that area, and to the west, a bastion protected a stepped passageway down to the plain. Secure access to a secret supply of water was also ensured as part of this expansion: in the lower citadel two openings in the inner face of the north-east part of the wall led to two parallel passages cut underground beneath the fortifications and thence to subterranean water cisterns.

Perhaps the same fears lay behind the abandonment of some of the buildings outside the walls at Mycenae at this time and the moving of workshops and storage facilities within the protective orbit of the fortifications at both Mycenae and Tiryns.

The palace on the acropolis at Athens had apparently first been fortified around the middle of the thirteenth century by rulers imitating the fortification systems of the Argolid citadels. At the end of the thirteenth century it too secured a water supply that was accessible from within its walls. As at Tiryns and Mycenae, the defences were modified to give access to an underground spring in a chamber shaped like a beehive and reached by a flight of steps dug down beneath the fortification walls.

A further piece of Mycenaean building may indicate that the Mycenaeans knew themselves to be in danger. Stretches of a great wall have been found, beginning on the shores of the Saronic Gulf and continuing westwards. This has been thought to be a massive defensive wall, built right across the Isthmus of Korinth to protect against a land attack from the north, and perhaps never completed. However, it is equally possible that it was not a defensive wall at all, but rather a retaining wall for a road, leading from the coast of the Saronic Gulf across to the main plateau of the Rachi and thence inland.

Some believe that a striking and very different indication of threat comes from the palace of Pylos. Lying on a low hill near the coast, it was particularly vulnerable. Any approach by land was difficult, as the palace was protected to the east and to the north by mountain ranges. An enemy could approach by land from the north along the west coast, but an easily defensible pass offered protection there. The greatest threat to the security of Pylos would be from the sea, a fact well recognized by the Pylians. Dramatic documentary evidence of their precautionary measures comes in a set of five Linear B tablets from

117. A subterranean water cistern was reached via an underground staircase from within the walls of Mycenae.

the palace headed 'Thus the watchers are guarding the coastal regions'. A total of 800 men are sent to the coast, which is divided into ten sections reaching from the Nedha river to the north and then down to Cape Akritsa before heading north again into the gulf of Messenia. Given the length of the coastline to be covered, 800 men would not be a sufficient defensive force but could provide an effective early warning system to alert the palace of an enemy approaching by sea. As we only have tablets from the last year of the palace we have no way of knowing if these watchmen were sent out on a regular basis, or whether they were in response to a specific threat at the time. What we do know, however, is that it was ultimately to no avail.

DESTRUCTIONS

Whatever the precautions taken by the Mycenaeans, nothing could save them from their fate. Around 1200 BC one after another of the mighty centres of Mycenaean Greece fell and were consumed by terrible fires which twisted and melted the very walls of the palaces. This same picture is seen elsewhere in the years around 1200 BC as great havoc was wrought across the lands of the eastern Mediterranean. Just as the palaces and citadels of the Mycenaeans fell, so did those of the empire of the Hittites in Anatolia and many urban centres of the Levant. This destruction horizon, which also brought to a close the New Kingdom in Egypt, heralded the end of the Bronze Age itself, ushering in a new age – that of Iron.[1]

At Mycenae and Tiryns the pattern of destruction was a complex one, confined not to one episode but perhaps to as many as three, occurring in the mid-thirteenth century, the end of the century and again in the early twelfth century. At Midea there is apparently evidence so far for a single episode at the end of the century, with a deposit of ash and burnt mudbrick walls showing intense fire. At all three sites there was clearly rebuilding and reoccupation in the twelfth century. But it was not only these three great fortresses that were to suffer in the Argolid: smaller sites such as Zygouries and Irea were also destroyed around 1200 BC; and elsewhere in the same region it appears that some places were simply abandoned, such as Berbati and Prosymna. Conversely, settlements like Asine, relatively unimportant in the thirteenth century, escaped unscathed and went on to flourish into the twelfth century.

Pylos, close to the sea and thus so vulnerable to attack, was sacked, burned and largely abandoned shortly after 1190 BC. As far as can be ascertained from the Linear B tablets found at the palace, it was in the early spring that this dreadful calamity befell the Pylians. Their attackers may well have come from the sea, despite the efforts of the watchers at the coast. The excavations at the site have found no bodies of its former inhabitants, suggesting they had perhaps been warned in time by the watchers and had been able to flee their palace before the enemy arrived. Two towns north-east of the palace, Malthi and Mouriatadha, were burned. The destruction of the palace at Pylos seems to have been accompanied by the desertion of many neighbouring sites, some of which were then reoccupied, albeit on a smaller scale, in the twelfth century. In the south-east of the Peloponnese, in Laconia, the site of the Menelaion was destroyed by fire around 1200 BC and not reoccupied, though some Laconian settlements continued to flourish, notably at Monemvasia, where a large necropolis of chamber tombs has been discovered.

Further north the picture of widespread destructions continues. In Boiotia the Kadmeion in Thebes was burnt down c.1200 BC and then reoccupied, and the end came also to Orchomenos and Gla, though at the latter at least this appears to have happened some thirty to forty years earlier. At Athens the acropolis has been so overbuilt by later structures that little remains of the Mycenaean era on which to evaluate the evidence for a possible destruction. However, what evidence there is shows no sign of a catastrophe and the site seems to have continued to prosper in the twelfth century. Athens, therefore, may have been one Mycenaean fortress that escaped the ravages of the end of the thirteenth century. Other lesser sites in the region also show continuity, such as that of Lefkandi (Xeropolis) on the island of Euboia. As at Athens, it appears that the Mycenaean palatial centre at Iolkos (Volos) survived the 1200 BC destructions, but was then burned down early in the twelfth century.

What caused the end of so many of the great centres of Mycenaean culture? This was no gradual decline, but a sudden, violent destruction. The causes must be sought, but the question is a complex one and there are no easy answers.

There are four main categories of argument: foreign invasion, internal strife, natural disasters and systems collapse. It is perfectly understandable that scholars have looked for a foreign invader. It seems clear from the great fortifications of the Argolid citadels themselves, expanded and strengthened in the middle of the thirteenth century and provided with a secure water supply at the end of it, that the Mycenaeans were prepared for attack.

A DORIAN INVASION

The so-called 'Dorian Invasion' is a persistently recurring theory, and one that is still repeated today in general books long after it has been recognized as untenable by the very great majority of Aegean scholars. The most extreme version envisages hordes of marauding northern tribes – often thought to have come from the Balkans – sweeping down in an invasive wave, conquering the Mycenaeans and establishing themselves in their stead, forming the bloodstock that gave us the Greeks of the Classical world. The decipherment of Linear B, showing that Greek speakers were already established in the area during the Mycenaean age, has negated some of these extremes, but why does the idea still persist?

Proponents of a Dorian invasion cite the tradition, enshrined in Classical Greek literature, of the 'return of the Heraklidai'. Thucydides tells us: 'Sixty years after the fall of Troy, the modem Boeotians were driven out of Arne by the Thessalians and settled in what is now Boeotia, but used to be called Kadmeis. Twenty years later the Dorians with the descendants of Herakles made themselves masters of the Peloponnese.' Such ancient sources do indeed write of 'Dorians' and connect them with population movements in the area, but the very concept of the 'return' of the Heraklidai surely implies that these were no alien people. The traditions of such movements of peoples do seem to reflect a certain degree of pressure from the north, but certainly do not support any idea of a marauding northern enemy. Herodotus is the only writer to state that the Dorians came from the north, from Thessaly, whilst the others see the Heraklidai as having originated in the Argolid and to be returning there. All the stories in the ancient sources of population movements at the end of the 'heroic age' show that the Classical Greeks saw them purely in terms of internal movements within Greece itself, not as foreign incursions.

The geographical distribution of different dialects of Greek, as they stood in Classical times, would seem to support the traditions of population shifts within Greece, both from west to east and from north to south, with consequent displacement of elements of the population. A study of epigraphy reveals five dialect groups that can be put into the two broad categories of East Greek and West Greek dialects. The East Greek group incorporates Attic-Ionic (Attica, Euboia, west coast of Asia Minor and the north and central islands of the Cyclades), Aeolic (Thessaly, Boiotia, Lesbos and the coast of north-west Asia Minor) and Arcado-Cypriot (Arcadia and Cyprus). The dialects of the West Greek group are Doric (spoken in the lands found on the coasts of the Peloponnese, such as the Argolid, Laconia and Messenia, and their colonies as well as on Crete and the southernmost Cyclades and the Dodecanese) and North West Greek (Phocis, Locris and Elis).

Attempts to detect dialects in the early Greek inscribed on the Linear B tablets of the Mycenaeans have found elements that indicate the presence of East Greek but not West Greek. This is used by some as an argument in favour of Doric being introduced by intrusive elements after the fall of the palaces. It is, however, explained by others in terms of an East Greek related dialect being that of the palace rulers, with Doric the dialect of the lower classes, as we will see later in this chapter.

In the earlier decades of this century, the destructions of the Mycenaean palaces, so demonstrable in the archaeological record, were tied up with legends and dialect groupings to give us the theory of the Dorian Invasion. However, as archaeological exploration continues and our understanding of the Mycenaeans grows ever more sophisticated, it has become steadily more apparent that such a simple correlation is untenable. If a great migratory invasion had indeed taken place, wiping out the Mycenaean world, we would have not only destructions of sites but also evidence of an intrusive alien culture. An intrusive group, which would after all have to be very numerous to quell and vanquish the Mycenaeans, would bring with it its own identifiable artefacts – pottery, for instance, and weapons – as well as leaving other traces such as new grave types. But we look in vain in the archaeological record for such invaders. When sifting through the ruins of the palaces of the Mycenaeans, we don't discover alien peoples living there after the destructions, nor do we find new settlements founded by them elsewhere.

There are, indeed, a few types of artefact thought to be new to the Mycenaean world at this time, argued by some to reflect the presence of newcomers. The Naue II type sword, for instance, is a European sword type seen as intrusive, but although prevalent in the twelfth century was in fact already carried by Mycenaean warriors in the thirteenth century BC before the destructions. They were, in addition, adopted first in the Peloponnese and on Crete, not in northern Greece, as one would expect if they had been carried in the hand of an invading enemy, encroaching from the north. Other weapons such as the socketed spearhead and the Pescheira dagger are foreign to Greece and do first appear at the time of the destructions, but do not appear in the Argolid and cannot, therefore, be associated with invaders sacking the palaces. Two types of large brooch, the violin bow fibula and the arched fibula, are common in twelfth-century contexts, but they, like the Naue II type sword, appear in Greece already in the thirteenth century. To be used as arguments for invading Dorians, such types of artefacts would need to be attested in the archaeological record suddenly at the time of the destructions, to be concentrated in date and to be geographically associated with the path of the invaders. None of these applies to the artefacts in question. Such innovations could most reasonably be explained as arriving as items of trade – good ideas and technical advances are likely to be readily adopted without needing to be imposed by an invading enemy force.

It remains now to see if there are any intrusive types of pottery that can be associated with such a force. Small amounts of pottery, both whole pots and sherds, thought to be intrusive have been identified at a few twelfth-century sites post-dating the destructions. Known as Rutter Ware, after the scholar who identified it, these pieces of handmade and burnished ware were manufactured locally, for instance at Korakou, and were thus taken as evidence of an intrusive population element. Further excavation of twelfth-century sites, however, such as at Kalapodi in north-central Greece, have shown that this type of pottery came into use very gradually and not suddenly with an influx of invaders.

Another element very central to a culture is its own burial customs, and the cist grave, appearing around the end of the thirteenth century and into the twelfth, is sometimes seen as evidence for foreign incursions. Cists were, it is noted, current in the thirteenth century in the north, in Epirus. However, the cist is a very simple and very basic grave form. It was common in the Middle Helladic period and attested throughout the Late Bronze Age in Greece, albeit sporadically. It became popular again in Greece in the twelfth century, especially in the Argolid and Attica. This resurgence of its popularity surely has less to do with invaders than to being a reaction to impoverishment and insecurity, especially as the grave goods found in such graves are purely Mycenaean. Communal forms of grave, such as the tholos and chamber tomb, required a great deal of effort to construct and were intended to be used for multiple burials, often spanning very many years. Under conditions of insecurity, people would be less likely to invest in this way in the future. In addition, the adoption of the cist grave in the twelfth century cannot be tied up with Dorian areas, as it was prevalent, for instance, in Athens.

In this search through the wave of destructions that hit the Mycenaeans, no trace of a wave of invaders from the north can be found. In fact the archaeological record shows the exact opposite. It is Mycenaeans who are living in the ruins of their palaces. It is Mycenaean pottery that we find in the pockets of reoccupation and Mycenaeans who we find buried in the tombs, identified as such by their grave goods. A final point needs to be stressed: if the Mycenaeans were brought down by an archaeologically invisible invasion, where did all these invaders go? The end of Mycenaean culture was followed, in the 'Dark Age', by dramatic depopulation, surely evidence for a great diaspora rather than an influx of large numbers of newcomers.

THE SEA PEOPLES

If we are to explain the demise of the Mycenaeans as being through enemy action, we have to find an enemy who left no trace, other than the destructions they caused. This would envisage bands of raiders overcoming and sacking Mycenaean sites and then withdrawing before they left any evidence of themselves in the archaeological record. These raider theories focus on the Sea Peoples, who were sea-borne warriors, probably largely Philistines, known to have caused havoc in the late thirteenth and early twelfth centuries in Cyprus, the Levant and the coast of Anatolia, and also in Egypt until crushed by the might of the pharaoh Rameses III around 1190 BC.

Was a raid by the Sea Peoples what the Pylians so feared? Despite keeping a watch over the sea, their city was sacked, burned and abandoned. Given the proximity of Pylos to the coast and the nature of the Sea Peoples as piratical raiders, one might envisage that this rich and undefended palace would present easy pickings. But the Sea Peoples are unlikely candidates for the devastation on the rest of the Greek mainland. The Mycenaeans in general do not seem to have felt under threat from the sea. Many of the so-called refuge sites, whose populations were swelled by displaced Mycenaeans from other areas in the early twelfth century, lay on or very close to the coast, such as Tiryns and the site of Lefkandi on the island of Euboia.

It is a tidy theory to try and tie up the troubles in the Mediterranean with those historically documented in Egypt, but there is no tangible evidence that the Sea Peoples ever did stray over to the Aegean. Some destructions in other coastal areas of the Mediterranean have been attributed to the Sea Peoples, but the role they played, even in the eastern Mediterranean – for example, in the fall of the Hittites – may have been overestimated. It is possible that displaced Mycenaeans, driven from their homes by the wave of destructions around 1200 BC, actually joined the ranks of the Sea Peoples and themselves became piratical raider warriors.

INTERNAL STRIFE

If the Mycenaeans were not attacked by a foreign enemy, could they perhaps have attacked each other? The myths and legends of Classical Greece are full of tales of strife between, and even within, dynasties. The legends that surround the palace of Thebes, for instance, point to some kind of power struggle between the Argolid and Boeotia. Could these stories have at their heart a memory of such rivalries in the Bronze Age? And could this internecine strife have brought about the demise of the Mycenaeans? It is of course possible that there were indeed fierce rivalries between the palaces, but we cannot use myth as

118. The Sea Peoples, defeated in battle around 1180 BC by Rameses III, carved in relief on the walls of a temple at Medinet Habu on the west bank of the Nile at Thebes.

history, and there is no supporting evidence from the archaeological record for this theory.

Another internal strife scenario suggests an insurrection by the lower classes. Certainly, an oppressed substratum of Mycenaean society is evident in the Linear B tablets, which reveal that the people of these Mycenaean states lived under a very controlled regime, with considerable numbers of slaves forming part of the economy. Some scholars studying the Greek inscribed on Linear B tablets believe that the lack of traces of Doric dialect in Linear B Greek, and its subsequent prevalence in the Peloponnese in the Classical period, is because Doric, or rather an early form of it, was spoken by the lower classes of Late Bronze Age Greece. Other factors pertaining to the destructions of the Mycenaean palaces make this an attractive, if still entirely speculative, theory. It would, for instance be far more feasible to bring down such heavily fortified citadels as Mycenae and Tiryns from within those great walls rather than from outside them. Also, it would explain why we do have destructions, but do not have any signs of intrusive elements.

NATURAL DISASTERS

Other explanations for the downfall of the Mycenaeans do not depend on the actions of man, but on the forces of nature. It has been argued that there was a great drought caused by climatic changes, resulting in large areas of Greece, from Messenia in the south to Epiros in the north, not getting enough rainfall. The consequent crop failure then led to famine, bringing about the collapse of the Mycenaean world. Pollen evidence, however, shows no sign of extreme climatic changes and the tablets at Pylos present a totally different picture, with many crops and numerous animals listed on them. The adoption of fibulae at this time – heavy brooches suitable for pinning thick woollen garments – has been cited as evidence that, if anything, it was getting colder rather than hotter. Another environmental theory blames over-exploitation of land by the centralized Mycenaean palaces, with pressure from the palace bureaucracies leading to mono-cropping of cereals and fields not left to lie fallow. This would leave the kingdoms vulnerable to even a short period of drought. Again, though, the Linear B tablets show no sign of drought or of famine.

Could some other natural catastrophe have caused such widespread destruction in the kingdoms of the Greek mainland? We know that the mainland and the islands of Greece have been bedevilled throughout their history by earthquakes, some of them so severe as, for instance, to have destroyed the Old Palaces on Crete. Over recent years a consensus has begun to emerge that there was indeed a terrible earthquake in the Argolid at the end of the thirteenth century. The excavators of the three great citadel sites of Mycenae, Tiryns and

Midea have all independently come to the conclusion that what destroyed their respective sites was this earthquake. At Mycenae the excavators have found what they consider to be unmistakable signs of severe earthquake damage around 1200 BC. The quake had been strong enough to actually twist and buckle the great walls, causing enormous damage and destruction both within the citadel and to houses outside the fortified acropolis. Not only had walls above ground at Mycenae collapsed, but their very foundations were damaged.

The nearby fortress of Tiryns also suffered severely around the end of the century. Not only were the buildings within the walls of destroyed, but the vast fortifications themselves were very badly damaged. Tiryns was later to be struck by a second earthquake, but of a far more localized nature as it does not appear to have affected Mycenae. Recent excavations at the citadel of Midea, the third of the Argolid fortresses, have again uncovered clear evidence of earthquake damage, with large numbers of huge blocks of stone having tumbled down from the fortifications, and buildings within the walls having collapsed. All three sites show that they were consumed by intense fire: scorching, ash layers, and walls and pottery deformed by the strength of the blaze are proof of this.

A single large earthquake could indeed have simultaneously struck the three citadels, which lie relatively near to each other in the Argive plain. Such an earthquake cannot, however, have destroyed all of the palaces and sites of the Mycenaeans at the end of the thirteenth century. It remains to question why, even given the ferocity of the earthquake, the Mycenaeans did not pick themselves up and start again. After all, when the Old Palaces on Crete were destroyed the Minoans went on to build new and more luxurious palaces, going from strength to strength. We will see that the Mycenaeans, although patching up parts of the palaces within the walls and continuing to inhabit Mycenae, Tiryns and Midea, did not recover, and the palace system collapsed, to be followed a hundred years later by the final decline of Mycenaean culture.

SYSTEMS COLLAPSE

The centralized structure of the Mycenaean kingdom allowed it to support a far larger population than the land could normally sustain. It is clear from Linear B tablets that life in the palaces was highly regulated, and that the Mycenaean palace élites controlled the day-to-day existence of their kingdoms to a minute degree. A complex redistributive system had been established, which marked a sharp divergence from the subsistence economy that had formed the basis of society in Greece before the development of Mycenaean culture at the beginning of the Late Bronze Age. If this system broke down, then the society it supported was in danger of collapsing; the people would have largely forgotten the ways of subsistence farming. Could the very sophistication of the life led by the Mycenaeans have been their downfall? Late Bronze Age Mycenaean sites had been demonstrably more numerous, larger and wealthier than those in the Middle Bronze Age, and once the palaces fell they could not be supported and the numbers of sites in the twelfth century declined rapidly.

No one single explanation will satisfactorily answer the question of what brought down the Mycenaean palaces. It seems that we need to find local answers for localized problems over a period of time at the end of the thirteenth century. Mycenae, Tiryns and Midea do all appear to have fallen because of a single great earthquake that shook the Argive plain around 1200 BC. Pylos, on the other hand, appears to have been vanquished by an enemy, probably attacked in a raid from the sea. Although we talk of the destructions taking place *c.*1200 BC, they are dated according to the rather loose chronological guidelines of pottery found in the ruins, and thus do not have to be envisaged as occurring simultaneously. The destruction horizon in which the palaces fell probably spanned a considerable number of years. What is clear, though, is that although localized factors may have been responsible for damaging or destroying different palaces, all of them were vulnerable, and were unable to recover from the various fates that befell them. A devastating earthquake in the Argolid, for instance, may have left other centres vulnerable and destabilized, perhaps disrupting trading routes on which travelled precious metals from the Laurion mines. Life for the Mycenaeans must have been very insecure and unstable in the closing years of the thirteenth century.

THE MYCENAEANS AFTER THE PALACES

The final century of the Late Bronze Age, around 1185 to 1065 BC, was to be the last century of the Mycenaeans, their society reeling under the series of blows that had brought down the might of its great citadels.[2] As we saw earlier in this chapter, it is Mycenaeans and not groups of foreign peoples that we find living amongst the shattered remnants of their former glory, rebuilding parts of great sites like Mycenae and Tiryns and swelling the ranks of those living in refugee sites. It is clear that there were far fewer Mycenaeans living on mainland Greece in the twelfth century than there had been in the years of the preceding palace era. The numbers and the size of their settlements show a dramatic decline. Some Mycenaeans sought refuge elsewhere, settling, for instance, on Cyprus and on the coast of the Near East – the beginnings of a great diaspora that was to reach its height at the end of the century in the final years of the Bronze Age.

Of those who stayed at home, some lived within former palaces, albeit on a diminished scale of opulence. Some palaces were never reoccupied after their destruction, notably Pylos, but others show clear evidence of being home to large and flourishing communities in the twelfth century. All three of the devastated Argolid citadels were reoccupied. At Mycenae a vigorous community lived on in areas of the palace, and at Midea the lower terraces at least were home to twelfth-century Mycenaeans. The lower town at Tiryns was very densely occupied in the years after the 1200 BC destructions, despite going on to suffer a second earthquake in the twelfth century. An area built up against the west wall of the lower town had rooms where there was evidence for the smelting of metal and a building of megaron type that contained some particularly fine terracotta figurines, probably one of the cult areas of the citadel.

Settlements which had been small and relatively unimportant in the palace years now became flourishing centres, with a large influx of new – but still Mycenaean – people from other stricken centres. Lefkandi, Perati, Achaia, Kephallenia and Ialysos on Rhodes, all sites with good access to the sea, prospered. Access to sea trading routes must have been ever more important as traders may well have been loath to travel into the hinterland of the Greek mainland in such times of insecurity and possible danger.

The life led by these twelfth-century Mycenaeans was rather different to that of earlier centuries. Even those palace sites that were reoccupied no longer functioned as palaces; as administrative and redistributive centres controlling an area. This is clear when one looks at the change of use of various areas of the palace sites from the thirteenth to the twelfth centuries. The great storage areas no longer function, as the palaces are not taking in, storing and redistributing crops produced in the region they once controlled. No trace of writing has been found in the post-destruction phases of the palaces: Linear B had been evolved to meet the demands of a complex bureaucracy, and the demise of that bureaucracy saw the end also of the script used to regulate it. Just as the need for writing had died, so apparently had much of the demand for luxuries. Many of the arts and skills of the previous centuries, such as the working of precious materials like ivory and fine stones, stopped with the destructions of 1200 BC.

In architectural terms, projects that required a corporate effort, such as Cyclopean masonry and monumental stone-built tombs, were discontinued. The communities at the former palace sites of Tiryns and Volos did undertake quite extensive building in the early twelfth century, but neglected the great Cyclopean walls of the citadels, allowing them to fall into disuse and disrepair. No new tholos tombs were built and it appears that even the existing ones were not used for any new

119. After an influx of Mycenaeans reached Cyprus in the twelfth century BC, very fine ivory carvings were made on the island with Mycenaean themes. This twelfth-century ivory of a warrior fighting a griffin is from Enkomi.

burials. Architectural refinements once fostered by the palace élites were lost to the Mycenaeans of this last century of the Bronze Age. Excavations of the prosperous settlement on the lower town at Tiryns, for instance, have uncovered no trace of fresco painting, which had been very much an art of the palaces.

The only hint from anywhere of a continuation of the art of fresco painting comes from a chamber tomb at Mycenae, where a stone stele was found, painted with a scene of marching warriors. The warrior ethos of the Mycenaeans thus still continued, even in these changed times, and warrior burials have been found of the early twelfth century, notably in regions to which Mycenaeans fled after the destructions of the end of the thirteenth century – Achaia, for instance, and Kephallenia. Those artefacts which were produced by these communities are still purely Mycenaean, and often of a very high standard.

Artistic expression is most clearly seen in the pottery styles of the twelfth century, which are important not simply for their artistic merit but also for the clear signs they give of a growth in regionalism. This regionalism, with different centres of the Mycenaean world producing identifiable styles, is in marked contrast to the uniform culture of the palace years. At Mycenae alone there were three distinct pottery styles – Close Style, Granary Style and Pictorial Style – whilst on Crete we have Fringe Style, and on the islands of the Cyclades, Octopus Style. Lefkandi on the island of Euboia has produced some very fine Pictorial Style pottery, most notably a large straight-sided alabastron endearingly decorated with a pair of griffins feeding their young in a nest.

Despite widespread and clear signs of decline, there were areas of Mycenaean Greece, notably Attica, which maintained a certain sophistication of lifestyle in the twelfth century. We saw earlier in this chapter that Athens may have escaped relatively unharmed by the destructions of 1200 BC. At Perati in Attica, a large cemetery of chamber tombs has been excavated. The contents of the graves included amber from the Baltic, a knife from Syria and scarabs and glass from Egypt, showing that this settlement at least was still tapping in to wide trading links. Lefkandi on the island of Euboia was very prosperous, as was Ialysos on Rhodes, which shows no trace of a 1200 BC destruction and appears to have received many refugees from less secure Mycenaean areas. The story of destructions was, however, not yet over. Even these pockets of continuing Mycenaean culture were not safe. Areas of the site of Mycenae, including the Granary, were devastated by fire towards the middle of the century and Tiryns was hit by a second earthquake. The palace at Iolkos was destroyed by fire at the beginning of the century and Lefkandi on Euboia, Miletos on the coast of Asia Minor and Emborio on the island of Chios all fell in flames.

The hundred years that were left to the Mycenaeans were littered sporadically with such localized disasters. But the Mycenaeans were finally not to go out as they came in, in a blaze of glory. Instead they simply fizzled out. Mycenaean culture had lost its heart, and just after 1100 BC the last vestiges of this great Bronze Age people were enveloped by the encroaching mists of the 'Dark Age'.

THE DARK AGE

With the onset of the Dark Age, the culture of the Mycenaeans came to an end. The Greeks learnt the working of iron from Cyprus, thus bringing to an end the Age of Bronze and ushering in that of Iron. Their life became very different from how it had been for much of the Mycenaean period and the picture that emerges out of the dark centuries is one of poverty and isolation. Depopulation had taken its toll, and the settlements of the Dark Age Greeks were, for the most part, small and scattered, their architecture characterized by a lack of monumentality and fine materials.[3]

These communities were isolated from the outside world and often from each other, and the regionalism that we saw emerging in the last century of the Bronze Age became even more marked. There were notable exceptions to this picture of unremitting gloom: occasional flashes of brilliance that illuminate the years of the Dark Age. Lefkandi, on the island of Euboia, for example, continued to look outwards, and for much of the Dark Age it flourished. But in general the life led in these small communities was simple, and although essential crafts, such as that of the potter, continued, the working of precious materials and the fine arts practised during the Mycenaean years were lost.

Amongst the skills lost was that of writing. Throughout the centuries of the Dark Age there is no trace anywhere in the Greek world of writing, and when the country once again becomes literate, in the latter half of the eighth century BC, an entirely different form of script is found. The syllabic script of the Mycenaeans was replaced by an alphabetic one, adapted by the Greeks from that already established by the Phoenicians. During the Dark Age, therefore, Greece was illiterate and without literacy there is no means of recording events – and thus no history.

11

Myth, Legend and the Trojan War

When Greece finally emerged out of its Dark Age, it did so not with a written history of what had gone before but with a network of myths and legends that had been passed down over the centuries from bard to bard. This oral tradition told tales of an heroic age and the great exploits of those who lived in it. Unfortunately, these poems survive today in mostly fragmentary form, sometimes only preserved as quotations in the works of later writers. The *Iliad* and the *Odyssey* are the only ones to have survived in anything like a complete form and recount certain episodes from the story of the Trojan War, in which the Greeks set sail and lay siege to Troy for ten years before finally gaining access to, and sacking, the city. Much of the lost network of poetry, myth and legend that tells the rest of the story was clearly, however, known to the Classical Greeks, who painted scenes from it on their pottery and used it as the theme of many of their tragedies.

It was the *Iliad* and the *Odyssey* that inspired Heinrich Schliemann to go in search of the Trojan War and its protagonists. His quest took him first to the mound of Hissarlik in the Trojan plain, where he found the lost city of Troy, and then on to the Greek mainland in search of the Homer's Achaean heroes, where he began the discovery of the Mycenaeans. Schliemann's faith in the historical accuracy of the poems was absolute, and it led to him to some of the most spectacular archaeological discoveries ever made, but to what extent was this belief justified?

We have already established that there was no writing in Greece for several hundred years, from around 1200 BC to the mid-eighth century BC, so the poems cannot in any real sense be history. Could they, though, be a record, however modified or embellished, of a real war fought between the Greeks and the Trojans back in the Late Bronze Age?

HOMER AND ORAL TRADITION

The answer to this question must begin with an understanding of the nature of the poems themselves as being products of an oral tradition.[1] The bard painted around 1200 BC on the wall of the megaron in the Mycenaean palace of Pylos, seated on a rock and playing a lyre,

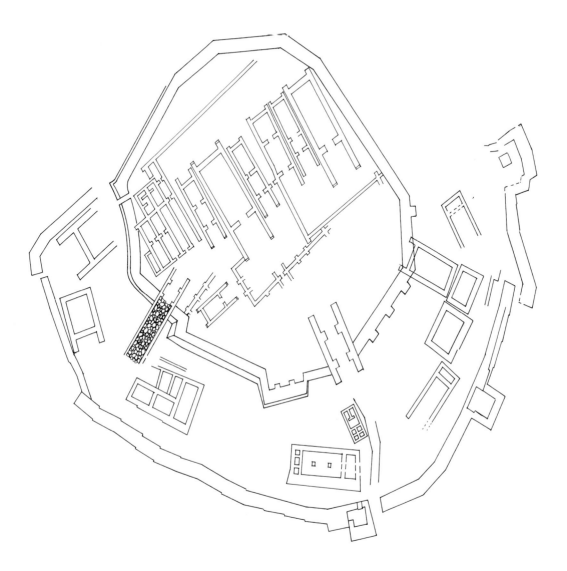

120. Plan of Troy, showing Troy II and Troy VI and VIIa.

belongs to the moment just before the Greeks lost the knowledge of writing. His successors will have sung tales of great kings, heroes and battles over the next few centuries from memory, passing them down over many generations. In the middle of the eighth century BC Greece once again became literate, having adopted an alphabetic script from the Phoenicians, and this enabled the network of poems to be eventually written down.

According to ancient tradition it was roughly at the same time (around the mid-eighth century) that Homer, who was said to have lived in one of the Ionian Greek colonies – perhaps Smyrna or Chios – composed his epic poems. Homer is believed to have been an oral poet, and if so then his works may have been written down in his lifetime, or relatively soon afterwards. References to him and his works exist from the fifth century: the earliest being found in Xenophanes and Heraklitos around 500 BC.

Much of the argument as to the historicity of the poems has been based on the reliability of oral tradition, a question that provokes polarised views. Can we use archaeology to provide an answer?

THE MYCENAEANS: HOMER'S ACHAEANS?

Well over a hundred years have now passed since Schliemann's great discoveries at Troy and the Mycenaean sites of the mainland. Our understanding of Mycenaean culture has grown since those early days, and the picture we now have is much more complete than that available to Schliemann late in the nineteenth century. Many scholars have studied the poems in an attempt to place the world they portray in time, and it is clear that they contain elements that range in date from the Late Bronze Age, through the Dark Ages to the eighth century BC.

What elements are there in the poems, then, that can be identified as survivals from an oral tradition that has its roots in the Late Bronze Age? Homer's kings lived in large, luxurious and brightly painted palaces, a setting now familiar to us from the Mycenaean world. Likewise, Homer's heroes had weapons of bronze at a time long after they had been largely replaced by ones of iron. Homer is here self-consciously heroizing his poems, setting them in a bygone age. Iron itself in the poems is recognized to be useful for tools and weapons, but is still viewed as essentially a metal of great value, even when unworked, looking back to a time when this was indeed the case – in the Bronze Age.

References to bronze body armour could date back to the Bronze Age, but could equally belong in Homer's own day, as examples have been found from both periods. Allusions in Homer to a corslet, or thorax, of bronze are paralleled in Linear B tablets, which have an ideogram for them. A full suit of Mycenaean sheet-bronze body armour (fig. 69), remarkably similar in form to that drawn on the tablets, was found in a small chamber tomb in the necropolis of Dendra near the citadel of Midea, complete with a boar's-tusk helmet and a pair of bronze greaves (leg-guards), the latter bringing to mind the Homeric epithet 'strong-greaved Achaeans'. Bronze body armour is, however, also known from the time of the poems' composition, for instance the fine bronze corslet and helmet discovered in a late eighth-century warrior grave at Argos.

Shields in Homer also appear to recall Mycenaean examples. The large tower-like shield, notably carried by Ajax in the *Iliad*, may be compared to the full-length shields used by the Mycenaeans. The lion hunt inlaid dagger from shaft grave IV at Mycenae shows hunters wearing two types of full-length body shield: the figure-of-eight and the tower shield, tall and rectangular in form (fig. 21). The shield of Ajax in the poem is furthermore described as being made of seven oxhides, and indeed those seen on the dagger have this patterning, as do fresco friezes of large figure-of-eight shields that are painted on the walls of the palaces of the Mycenaeans

Several individual objects detailed in the *Iliad* and the *Odyssey* clearly belong to the world of the Mycenaeans. Perhaps the most striking example is the highly prized helmet described in the *Odyssey*: 'Meriones gave to Odysseus a bow and a quiver and about his head he set a helm wrought of hide, and with many a tight-stretched thong was it made stiff within, while without the white teeth of a boar of gleaming tusks were set thick on this side and that, well and cunningly, and within was fixed a lining of felt.' This constitutes a very accurate account of the Mycenaean boar's-tusk helmet, known from actual examples and depictions spanning the entire Late Bronze Age, but going out of use at the end of it.

Similarly, the massive shield made for the hero Achilles by the smith-god Hephaistos is created from bronze, tin, silver and gold and decorated with many pictorial scenes. The vivid description of this shield is thought to reflect a memory of the Mycenaean art of inlaying bronze with cut-outs in precious metals. This technique was used to make miniature scenes of figures, animals and abstract and floral motifs, for instance on daggers of the Shaft Grave Era and on a variety of vessels.

More interesting perhaps than this matching of objects is where we find certain aspects of life in the poems that we are familiar with from the archaeological record. Elements of the funeral rites described in the poems certainly do echo those uncovered during excavations of Mycenaean tombs. The most complete account comes in Book XXIII of the *Iliad* with the description of the funeral of Patroklus. The poet tells us that the body of Patroklus was laid on a large funeral pyre, upon which were then sacrificed four horses, two dogs and twelve Trojan captives. The pyre was then set alight and, once the body was burned, the fire was extinguished with wine and the ashes and bones of the hero were gathered up and put in a gold jar. The bones of the hero were easily distinguishable from those of the sacrificial victims dedicated to him because his lay in the centre of the pyre and theirs to one side.

The sacrificing of horses, or other equids, is attested sporadically at tholos tombs of the Late Bronze Age in Greece, such as at Marathon in Attica. They were usually placed in pairs lying in the dromos (entrance-way) of the tomb, in front of the doorway to the burial chamber. Bones of dogs have also been found at Mycenaean burials of high status, presumably sacrificed to accompany their erstwhile master in death. In a pit dug in the floor of the tholos tomb at Dendra, inside the burial chamber but close to the doorway, were found dog bones mixed up with human ones. It may be that they both had been lying in the chamber from an earlier burial, had become intermingled and were cleared away into a pit when the tomb was prepared for subsequent use. It is, however, possible that the human bones found with those of the dog can be counted amongst the rare instances of what may be human sacrifice at Mycenaeans tombs. These, known for example at Mycenae and Argos, usually involved a skeleton found under the packing of stones blocking the doorway to the burial chamber, or lying just above the level of the doorway in soil used to fill the dromos. In one instance a total of six skeletons lay at various levels in the soil fill in front of the door.

The form in which the remains of the dead were interred, though, was very different at a Homeric burial: in the poems, Homer had his heroes cremated, whilst the Mycenaeans almost uniformly practised inhumation. Mycenaean cremations were extremely rare until the closing years of their culture. The rite of cremation described in the poems thus belongs to a post-Bronze Age phase of the transmission of the poems. A closer parallel for the kinds of rites seen in the funeral of Patroklus is found in the hero burial of the tenth century at Lefkandi on the island of Euboea. Here the ashes of a cremated hero had been found placed in a bronze cauldron and he was placed in his tomb accompanied by several skeletons of sacrificed horses and the inhumation of a woman. The latter had apparently been buried at the same time, richly dressed in gold jewellery and with an ivory-handled knife lying next to her head. There is a strong possibility that she, along with the horses, had been sacrificed at the time of the cremation burial.

The relation of such burial rites found in the ground to those described in the poems is a complex one. Horse and human sacrifice were not practised by the eighth-century Greeks of Homer's day, and the poems may therefore be recording a reminiscence of such rites practised at some other period of the poems' transmission, reflecting perhaps Mycenaean burials or ones such as that of tenth-century Lefkandi. A group of burials from eighth- and seventh- century Salamis on Cyprus share elements in common with the burial of Patroklus in the *Iliad*. The leitmotif of the tombs was horse sacrifice, and in one instance at least there was clear evidence of human sacrifice. One of the burials was a cremation in a bronze cauldron, though the others were inhumations. They have been interpreted as the people of Salamis imitating Homeric rituals, but are equally likely to be part of a sporadic tradition of hero burials, incorporating sacrificial elements.

After the funeral of Patroklus, games were held in his honour, including a chariot race, a foot race, a sport that seems to have been a combination of boxing and wrestling, hand-to-hand combat and a spear-throwing competition. The painted coffins from the Mycenaean cemetery at Tanagra in Boiotia include examples that appear to depict funeral games, indicating that such rites go back to the Bronze Age (see p.168). The mourning scenes on these coffins bear a remarkable resemblance in many respects to those painted on Late Geometric funerary vases of the late eighth century.

On a yet more fundamental level, can it be said that the political geography of the Homeric world reflects that of the Mycenaeans? The poems are set in a world that has Mycenae and its king, Agamemnon, in a position of loose hegemony over the other kingdoms. If we look to archaeology, is this the picture that emerges from the ground from the Late Bronze Age? From archaeology it is clear that Mycenae was exceptionally rich and powerful, but other than that there is nothing to indicate that its king held sway over the rest of the Mycenaean kingdoms. It has been thought that Tiryns, lying so close by, was under the dominance of Mycenae in some way, but Linear B tablets found there fairly recently offer no evidence of this. Likewise the archive found at Pylos, which has been extensively studied, gives no indication that the king of that palace owed allegiance to anyone or anywhere else.

The most comprehensive description of the political geography of the world of the poems comes in the 'Catalogue of Ships', a long and detailed passage in Book II of the *Iliad*.[2] This Catalogue details the battle line-up of the Greek forces, listing the towns, settlements and regions of Greece and the names of their legendary leaders and how many ships they sent to fight at Troy. The passage sits rather oddly in the *Iliad*, the action of which is set towards the end of the ten years of siege. It would fit more naturally near the beginning of the cycle of stories that told the whole story of the Trojan War, when the ships set out from Aulis, and therefore may well have been transplanted from another part of the epic cycle into the poem.

The 178 geographical names listed in the Catalogue cover almost all the areas of Greece. Many of the sites which appear wealthy and important in the Catalogue were indeed so in Mycenaean times and not in Homer's day. The palace of Pylos, famous as the home of the legendary king Nestor, sent many ships, but was in Homer's time a small and unimportant place. Similarly, descriptions in the Catalogue have led people to go in search of some of the sites mentioned and using clues given in it have identified the ruins of hitherto unknown important Mycenaean settlements.

Another striking feature of the Catalogue is that it appears to be Boiotia-centric and some scholars have argued that it was compiled at a time when the palace of Thebes was at its height. Thebes, so important in Greek myth and legend, is now proven through archaeological evidence to have been a rich and powerful palace. In the 1990s a large cache (some 250) of Linear B tablets was found there. These tablets belong to the palace archive of the Kadmeia, which was destroyed by fire around 1200 BC. Much interesting geographical information on the extent of the kingdom of Thebes has been gleaned from them and they show that the palace not only ruled the territory of Boiotia but also the strategically important island of Euboia. Thus Thebes appears to have controlled a far larger area than any other palace, even than Mycenae itself.

Interestingly, as work on the tablets from the Kadmeia progresses, more correspondences with the Catalogue of Ships are revealed. Amongst the thirty place names on them are Peteon, Eleon and Hyle, which all appear together on a line of the Catalogue as part of the Boiotian section. Eutresis (another place in the Catalogue also mentioned in the tablets), which has been identified and excavated, was destroyed in the thirteenth century BC and abandoned until around 600 BC and thus was known in the Bronze Age but not in Homer's own time.

The Catalogue, then, delineates what is apparently a fairly accurate picture of the geography of Mycenaean Greece. But even it is not without its anomalies: parts of it imply recognition of much later, post Bronze Age, political realities, such as the references to Cretans from Gortyn, which as far as we know was not settled until after the end of the Bronze Age.

As these tales were sung from bard to bard throughout the generations, they have retained something of their Bronze Age roots, albeit incorporating elements from subsequent centuries through which they passed. Can the poems have also kept a memory of a real conflict between the Greeks and the Trojans? Can we answer the question: is the Trojan War myth or history?

TROY VI AND VIIA

Schliemann's belief in the historicity of the Trojan War led him to discover Troy. As we now know, though, he dug down more than a thousand years too deep, driving his great trench through the levels where one might look for the Troy of the poems, and reaching Troy II (2600–2400 BC). Subsequent excavations at the site have identified two levels of the city, Troy VI and Troy VIIa, which between them spanned the years from around 1700–1200 BC and were thus contemporary with the culture of the Mycenaeans in Late Bronze Age Greece.[3] Both Troy VI and Troy VIIa have of course been thoroughly scrutinized for any clues that they might have been besieged and sacked at any point in their history. Mycenaean pottery has been found in quantities in both levels, demonstrating that the people of Troy and the Mycenaeans were in trading contact. Was there any evidence, though, of less friendly contact – indeed, of a war?

Manfred Korfmann began work at Troy in 1988 and for the first time an archaeologist who had worked extensively in Turkey (rather than Greece) was directing at the site. He was interested in Troy as an Anatolian site and was not intent on proving the historicity of the *Iliad*. As his excavations progressed, however, he made some extraordinary discoveries.

The great walls of Troy VI enclosed a town of wide streets, palatial buildings and fine, spacious houses. The citadel, however, although architecturally sophisticated and monumental, had seemed small for such an important site. Korfmann's excavations were to reveal that the city was in fact far larger than had ever been imagined. Geo-magnetic imaging uncovered the fact that Troy VI did not consist simply of the fortified area, but was surrounded by an extensive lower town spreading out on the plain below the citadel, home to as many as 6,000 to 10,000 inhabitants. Traces of a mighty city wall made of mud-brick on stone foundations were found, as was a large ditch (hewn out of the rock) encircling the lower town. Deep and wide and with walls on

121. The stone fortification walls of Troy VI.

both sides, further protecting the town, this defensive ditch enclosed an area of 200,000 sq m (some 2,000 acres); a second ditch was subsequently dug 100 m (109 yards) further out, perhaps as the town expanded.

Troy was clearly a large and important regional centre – an Anatolian city that must have derived its great wealth and power from its standing as a mighty trading centre. The bay of Beşik, some 8 km (5 miles) to the south-west of Troy appears to have been the city's harbour and Troy must have taken full advantage of its extraordinarily strategic position. The winds and currents prevalent in the Dardanelles could condemn ships to long periods in harbour waiting for favourable conditions in which to make the arduous journey into the Black Sea. Likewise it was the last safe anchorage before making the journey, so even in favourable conditions ships would need stop there to stock up on the necessary food, water and other provisions. This would have brought immense wealth to the city, a factor that is evident as far back as Troy II.

Troy VI, then, would seem a suitable candidate for the legendary city of Priam and Hecuba, as described in the poems. But it is now known to have been destroyed around 1300 BC by a great earthquake and not by siege or sack by an enemy. Troy VIIa was built on the earthquake-damaged ruins of Troy VI, and it lasted for roughly a century before being destroyed itself around 1180 BC. When we look at this city, the conditions under which its population lived were clearly different to those of the preceding one. Now we see its people living crammed within the walls of the citadel, living in houses huddled back to back and with *pithoi* (large storage jars), sunk into the floors of the buildings. It looks like a city under siege. Hastily buried bodies, quantities of arrowheads and spearheads found in the ruins, and piles of stone slingshots lying in the streets waiting to be fired at the enemy show that the Trojans put up a fierce fight. We have no way of knowing how long they withstood the siege, but the city finally fell to its attackers and was sacked around 1180 BC.

The city built subsequently, Troy VIIb, shows signs of an influx of new people, with pottery types from the Balkans. But who was the enemy? Nothing has yet been found in the ruins of Troy to identify those who sacked the city. Could the enemy have been the Mycenaeans, thus corroborating Homer's tale? Is there any evidence from elsewhere that might help us put together a picture of what really happened?

To try and answer this question we need first to look back to the Greek mainland, to what was happening there at the time when Troy was sacked. The picture is similar: at roughly the same time, the mainland suffered terrible destructions, with Pylos perhaps sacked from the sea and all three Argolid citadels falling in the face of a great earthquake.

Our difficulty here is in trying to decide whether Troy fell first, or the Mycenaean citadels, or whether these events happened simultaneously. Our relative chronology for these events is based on pottery styles. The same pottery is found in the ruins of Troy VIIa and the destructions in Greece, but as the pottery covers a fairly broad time span they could have happened as much as twenty years apart.

If we envisage Troy being destroyed first, then it is feasible, but still only a hypothesis, that the Mycenaeans could have set sail, lay siege to Troy and then come home before their own palaces fell. The securing of water supplies from within the citadel walls might then be seen as a measure taken in fear of reprisals. If it was the other way round, and the Mycenaean palaces fell before Troy, then Mycenaeans displaced from their own world may still have sacked the city, the oral tradition then connecting the glory days of the great palaces to a raid that belonged to a post-palatial era. These are both possible scenarios, but they are still only guesswork.

TROY IN THE HITTITE TEXTS

And here we must look back to Troy, as an Anatolian city belonging to an Anatolian world, to see if there is anything in the texts of the Hittite kings that might corroborate a Greek legend.[4]

Excavations at the Hittite capital Hattusa uncovered the imperial archive, documents that chronicle the history of the empire from around 1460 to 1190 BC. Soon after the script was deciphered scholars reading the texts discovered a treaty between the Hittite king Muwattalli II (1290–1271 BC) and Alaksandu of Wilusa. The treaty included, as was usual in such documents, a summary of the relations thus far between Wilusa and Hattusa, dating back to the time of king Tudhalija (1420–1400 BC) and so recounting a history of some 150 years. It also refers further back in time to a military conquest of Wilusa by Hattusa, perhaps as much as 300 years earlier. Since this first reference was discovered, other mentions of Wilusa have been identified in the Hittite texts. Amidst mounting speculation the question was asked: could it be that Wilusa is in fact one and the same as Ilios (Wilios in early Greek dialect), the other name for Troy in the Homeric epics?

But where was Wilusa? To identify Wilusa as (W)ilios, it needed to be located within the political geography of the Hittite world. A major breakthrough came with the discovery in Hattusa of a bronze tablet dating to reign of Tudhalija IV (1240–1215 BC) which gave information on countries to the west and north-west of Asia Minor, including an area in the latter, namely Wilusa. But could it be located even more exactly than that? In 1997 rock-cut figures of rulers accompanied by hieroglyphic Luwian inscriptions in the Karabel pass near Izmir finally gave up their secret: the inscriptions referred to the land of Mira, which was known to share borders with Seba, hence by inference clearly placing Wilusa in the Troad.

Here archaeology stepped in to corroborate the identification of Wilusa with Troy. The Alaksandu treaty had invoked the gods of Wilusa and the subterranean watercourse of Wilusa. During the 1997–8 excavation season at Troy, Korfmann discovered this very watercourse – a complex system of a reservoir, overflow tanks and channels – dated by scientific stone-dating methods to the beginning of the third millennium.

From Troy itself the only form of writing found so far is a hieroglyphic Luwian reversible seal made of bronze. The discovery of this Luwian seal at Troy, written in one of the languages of the Hittite Empire, indicates that there may have been a long-standing connection between the Great King at Hattusa and the ruler of Wilusa. What form this relationship took before the reign of Muwattalli II (1290–72 BC) is not clear, but with the Alaksandu treaty Wilusa became a vassal of the Hittite king. The last mention of Wilusa in the archives dates to the final years of the Hittite empire and was written during the reign of Tuhalija IV (1240–1215 BC) to another ruler as yet unidentified. Known as the Millawanda letter, it implies that the ruler of Wilusa has been deposed and the Great King is asking the help of the recipient to restore him to his throne.

HITTITES AND AHHIJAWANS

There is by now wide consensus that the name in the Hittite texts for mainland Greece is Ahhijawa and that it refers to a land which encompasses territory on the mainland, some of the islands and cities established on the coast of Asia Minor, most notably Miletos (MIllawanda in the Hittite texts).[5] Where the land of Ahhijawa was ruled from is still debated, with some scholars favouring Mycenae, and others Thebes.

It is clear that the relationship between the Hittites and the Ahhijawans did not always run smoothly, as one might expect from the two great lands with conflicting interests, especially along the Asia Minor coast. A letter found in the imperial archive at Hattusa was written not long after 1300 BC by a Hittite vassal king, Manatarbarhunta of Seba, to the then Hittite king Muwattalli II. He was writing to complain about the activities of a man called Pijamaradu, operating out of Millawanda (the Mycenaean colony of Miletos), who had been causing problems in Wilusa. The king of Seba went to the aid of Wilusa and asked for the help of the Hittite king. Muwattalli sent reinforcements but before they could reach Wilusa Pijamaradu had already raided the island of Lezba (Lesbos) and carried off craftsmen to Millawanda.

That Pijamaradu continued to be an aggressive and disruptive influence in the region for decades is made clear by other references to his activities, notably a letter written by the Hittite king Hattusili III (1265–1240 BC) to the King of Ahhijawa in the mid-thirteenth century

BC. Known as the Tawagalawa letter, it asks the king of Ahhijawa to restrain Pijamaradu and stop him from attacking Wilusa and Lesbos. Apparently the Hittite king couldn't capture him because he kept fleeing by ship to Ahhijawa. And there is now archaeological evidence from Miletos (Millawanda) that control of the city passed from the Greeks to the Hittites in the mid-thirteenth century, presumably in the context of this conflict.

The relationship between the Hittites and Ahhijawans was to deteriorate still further. In 1220 BC the Hittite king Tudhalija IV made a treaty with one of his vassal kings, Sausgamuwa of Amarru (a kingdom in northern Lebanon), in which Amarru was obliged to impose a trade embargo on Assyria (a powerful military rival with whom Hatti was at war) and to prevent the Assyrians from trading with Ahhijawa. Ahhijawa was clearly not only a security threat to Hittite lands, but also an economic one

CONCLUSION

The texts, then, reveal a history of potential conflict over Wilusa spanning several decades of the thirteenth century, in a context of military and economic rivalries. But to date there is no mention of the city being besieged and sacked, by the Greeks or anyone else. To go back to the wider picture, it was of course not only Troy that fell in Anatolia and the east at that time, but city after city and empire after empire, eventually bringing to an end the Bronze Age in that region, just as it ended in Greece. A vivid evocation of life in the beleaguered cities of the coast comes from Ugarit, where a cuneiform tablet, found still in its oven waiting to be baked, has written on it a letter from the king of Ugarit to the king of Cyprus, telling him of the burning of his towns by a sea-borne enemy.

Such raids are usually attributed to the Sea Peoples, who, according to Egyptian records, attacked the great cities of western Anatolia early in the twelfth century BC, laying waste the lands of Arzawa and the Hittites before going south, where they were defeated by Rameses III in 1180 BC. Could then the Sea Peoples have been responsible for the sack of Troy? And, indeed, might not displaced Mycenaeans themselves have been an element of these Sea Peoples, who appear to have been piratical warrior raiders of several nationalities.

Archaeology has given us a sack of Troy around 1180 BC, and in the form of the Hittite tablets has given us its Anatolian name, Wilusa, and a context of conflicts between Greeks and Hittites. What archaeology has not yet done, and perhaps never will, is tell us who the attackers were. That *a* Trojan War is history and not simply myth has been established. Whether *the* Trojan War is fact remains an open question.

Timeline

2300 BC:	Break in archaeological record; destructions at sites like Lerna
2000 BC:	Start of the Middle Bronze Age (Middle Helladic)
1600 BC:	Start of Late Bronze Age (Late Helladic)
1600–1450 BC:	The Shaft Grave Era; burials in Grave Circle A, Mycenae
1540 BC	The eruption of Thera
1450 BC:	Destructions on Crete
1375 BC:	Tiryns fortified
1350 BC:	Mycenae acropolis fortified
1300 BC:	Ulu Burun shipwreck
1250 BC	Mycenae citadel expanded and Lion Gate built
Just before 1200 BC:	Secure water supplies built at Mycenae, Tiryns and Athens
1200:	Destructions of the Mycenaean palaces
Roughly the same time:	Fall of Troy
1200–1080 BC:	Post-palatial era
1080 BC:	Start of the Dark Age

Notes

CHAPTER 1

1 Thucydides, *History of the Peloponnesian War*, I, 9; I, 10.
2 Euripides, *Heracles*, 944.
3 Pausanias, *Guide to Greece*, XI, 16, 4; XI, 27, 7.
4 Calder, W. and Traill, D. (eds), *Myth, Scandal and History: the Heinrich Schliemann controversy and a First Edition of the Mycenae Diary* (Detroit, 1986); Easton, D. F., 'Schliemann's Ausgrabungen in Troia', in Cobet, J. and Patzet, B. (eds), *Archaologie und historische Erinnerung* (Essen, 1992); Fitton, J. L., *The Discovery of the Greek Bronze Age* (London, 1995).
5 Schliemann, H., *Troy and its Remains* (London, 1875); *Ilios: the City and Country of the Trojans* (London, 1880); *Troja: Results of the Latest Researches* (London, 1884).
6 Schliemann, H., 'Exploration of the Boeotian Orchomenos', *JHS* 2 (1881), 122–63.
7 Schliemann, H., *Tiryns: the Prehistoric Palace of the Kings of Tiryns* (London, 1886).
8 Warren, P. and Hankey, V., *Aegean Bronze Age Chronology* (Bristol, 1989).
9 Manning, S., *A Test of Time: the Volcano of Thera and the Chronology and History of the Aegean and East Mediterranean in the mid Second Millennium* BC (Oxford, 1999).

CHAPTER 2

1 Ventris, M. and Chadwick, J., *Documents in Mycenaean Greek* (Cambridge, 1973); Chadwick, J., *Linear B and Related Scripts* (London, 1987); Hooker, J. T., *Linear B: an Introduction* (Bristol, 1980).
2 Caskey, J. L. and Blackburn, E.T., *Lerna in the Argolid* (Athens, 1997).
3 Dietz, S., *The Argolid at the Transition to the Mycenaean Age* (Copenhagen, 1991).

CHAPTER 3

1 Mylonas, G., *Grave Circle B at Mycenae* (Athens, 1973); *Mycenae and the Mycenaean Age* (Princeton, 1966).
2 Musgrave, J. H., Neave, R. A. H. and Prag, J., 'Seven faces from Grave Circle B at Mycenae', *BSA* 90 (1995) 107–36; Prag, J. and Neave, R. A. H., *Making Faces* (London, 1999).
3 Schliemann, H., *Mycenae* (New York, 1880).

CHAPTER 4

1 Detailed bibliographies for Shaft Grave Era topics can be found in Dickenson, O. T. P. K., *The Aegean Bronze Age* (Cambridge, 1994).
2 Davis, E., *The Vapheio Cups and Aegean Gold and Silver Ware* (Ann Arbor, 1973)
3 Morgan, L., *The Miniature Wall Paintings of Thera* (Cambridge, 1988).

CHAPTER 5

1 Marinatos, S., 'The volcanic destruction of Minoan Crete', *Antiquity* XIII, 425–39.
2 Fitton, J. L., *Minoans* (London, 2002), 31–6.
3 *Thera and the Aegean World. Proceedings of the Second International Scientific Congress* (2 vols; London, 1978 and 1980); *Thera and the Aegean World. Proceeding of the Third International Scientific Congress* (London, 1990).
4 Rehak, P., 'Aegean breechcloths, kilts and the Keftiu paintings', *AJA* 100, 35–51.
5 Boardman, J. and Palmer, L., *On the Knossos Tablets* (Oxford, 1963); Popham, M. R., 'The final destruction of the palace at Knossos: seals, sealings and pottery: a reconsideration', in Driessen, J. and Farnoux, A., *La Crète Mycénienne* (Athens, 1997).

CHAPTER 6

1 Iakovides, S. E., *Late Helladic Citadels on Mainland Greece* (Leiden, 1983); Loader, N. C., *Building in Cyclopean Masonry, with Special Reference to the Mycenaean Fortifications on Mainland Greece* (Göteborg, 1998).
2 Hiesel, G., *Späthelladische hausarchitektur* (Mainz, 1990); Küpper, M., *Mykenische architektur* (Espelkamp, 1996).
3 Immerwahr, S. A., *Aegean Painting in the Bronze Age* (Pennsylvania, 1990).
4 French, E. (ed.), *Excavations at Mycenae 1939–1955 by A. J. B. Wace and others* (London, 1979); French, E., *Mycenae: Agamemnon's Capital* (Stroud, 2002); Iakovides, S. and French, E. B., *Archaeological Atlas of Mycenae* (Athens, 2005).
5 Jansen, A. G., *A Study of the Remains of Mycenaean Roads and Stations of Bronze Age Greece* (Lewiston, NY, 2002).
6 For detailed bibliography on recent excavations at

Tiryns see Shelmerdine (2001: see further reading), 335.

7　For detailed bibliography on recent excavations at Midea see Shelmerdine (2001), 335–7.

8　Davis, J. L. (ed.), *Sandy Pylos: an Archaeological History from Nestor to Navarino* (Austin, 1998); Lolos, Y. G. *The Capital of Nestor and its Environs* (Athens, 1998); Shelmerdine (2001), 337–9.

9　For the new Linear B tablets from Thebes see resume and bibliography in Shelmerdine (2001), 355–6.

10　Holland, L. B., 'The strong house of Erechtheus', *AJA* 28 (1924), 142–69; Mountjoy, P.A., *Mycenaean Athens* (Goteborg, 1995); Shelmerdine (2001), 339–40.

11　Barber, E. J. W., *Prehistoric Textiles* (Princeton, 1991).

CHAPTER 7

1　Gale, N., *Bronze Age Trade in the Mediterranean* (Goteborg, 1991).

2　Mountjoy, P., *Mycenaean Pottery: An Inroduction* (Oxford, 1993).

3　Morgan, L., *The Miniature Wall Paintings of Thera* (Cambridge, 1988)

4　Yalcin, U., Pulak, C. and Slotta, R., *Das Schiff von Uluburun: Welthandel vor 3000 Jahren* (Bochum, 2005).

5　Davies, W. V. and Schofield, L. (eds), *Egypt, the Aegean and the Levant: Interconnections in the Second Millennium BC* (London, 1995).

6　Cline, E. H., *Sailing the Wine-Dark Sea: International Trade and the Late Bronze Age Aegean* (BAR International Series, 1994).

7　Harding, A. F. *The Mycenaeans and Europe* (London, 1984); Harding, A. F. and Hughes-Brock, H., 'Amber in the Mycenaean world', *BSA* 68 (1974), 145–72.

CHAPTER 8

1　Bennet, J., 'The Linear B archives and the kingdom of Nestor,' in Davis, J. (ed.), *Sandy Pylos: an Archaeo-logical History from Nestor to Navarino* (Austin, 1998).

2　Bucholz H-G. and Wiesner, J. (eds), *Archaeoloica Homerica. Kriegswesen, Teil I: Schutzwaffen und Wehrbauten* (Gottingen, 1997).

3　Crouwel, J. and Morel, J., *Chariots and Other Means of Land Transport in Bronze Age Greece* (Amsterdam, 1983).

4　Schofield, L. and Parkinson, R. B., 'Of helmets and heretics: a possible representation of Mycenaean warriors on a papyrus from el-Amarna', *BSA* 89 (1994), 157–70.

5　Peltenberg, E., 'Greeting gifts and luxury faience: a context for orientalizing trends in Late Mycenaean Greece', in Gale, N. (ed.), *Bronze Age Trade in the Mediterranean* (Jonsered, 1991); Betancourt, P. and Laffineur, R. (eds), *Teyvn: Craftsmen, Craftswomen and Craftsmanship in the Aegean Bronze Age* (Liege, 1997).

CHAPTER 9

1　A useful update with bibliography can be found in Shelmerdine (2001) 362–72.

2　Hägg, R. and Marinatos, N. (eds), Sanctuaries and Cults in the Aegean Bronze Age (Athens, 1981); Rutkowski, B., *Cult Places of the Aegean* (New Haven and London, 1986); Whittaker, H., *Mycenaean Cult Buildings* (Bergen, 1997); Renfrew C., *The Archaeology of Cult: the Sanctuary at Phylakopi* (London, 1985).

3　Chadwick, J., *The Mycenaean World* (Cambridge, 1976).

4　Cavanagh, W., 'Innovation, conservation and variation in Mycenaean funerary rituals', in Branigan, K. (ed.), *Cemetery and Society in the Aegean Bronze Age* (Sheffield, 1998); Hägg, R. and Nordquist G. C. (eds), *Celebrations of Death and Divinity in the Bronze Age Argolid* (Stockholm, 1990).

5　Immerwahr, S., 'Death and the Tanagra larnakes', in Carter, J. B. and Morris, S. M. (eds), *The Ages of Homer* (1995).

CHAPTER 10

1　An excellent resume of the destructions and their possible causes, together with detailed bibliography, can be found in Shelmerdine (2001), 372–6.

2　Desborough, V. R., *The Last Mycenaeans and their Successors: an Archaeological Survey c. 1200–1000 BC* (Oxford, 1964).

3　Snodgrass, A. M., *The Dark Age of Greece* (Edinburgh, 1971).

CHAPTER 11

1　Kirk, G. S. (ed.), The *Language and Background of Homer* (Cambridge, 1964); Parry, A. (ed.), *The Making of Homeric Verse: the Collected Papers of Milman Parry* (Oxford, 1971); Finley, M., *The World of Odysseus* (2nd edn, Harmondsworth, 1979); Hood, M. S. F., 'The Bronze Age context of Homer', in Carter, J. B. and Morris, S. P. (eds), *The Ages of Homer* (Austin, 1995); Bennet, J., 'Homer and the Bronze Age', in Morris, I. and Powell, B. (eds), *A New Companion to Homer* (Leiden, 1997).

2　Latacz, J., *Troy and Homer: Towards a Solution of an Old Problem* (Oxford, 2004), 219–38.

3　Blegen, C. W. et al., *Troy III: The Sixth Settlement* (Princeton, 1953); *Troia. Traum oder Wirklichkeit* (see further reading).

4　McQueen, J. G., *The Hittites and their Contemporaries in Asia Minor* (London, 1986); Bryce, T., *Life and Society in the Hittite World* (Oxford, 2002); Latacz, J. (op. cit., n.2).

5　Bryce, T. 'Ahhiyawans and Mycenaeans – an Anatolian viewpoint.' *OJA* 8, 279–310; Latacz, J. (op. cit., n.2), 120–36.

Further reading

GENERAL

Chadwick, J., *The Mycenaean World* (Cambridge, 1976)

Fitton, J. L., *The Discovery of the Greek Bronze Age* (London, 1995)

French, E., *Mycenae: Agamemnon's Capital* (Stroud, 2002)

Higgins, R., *Minoan and Mycenaean Art* (London, 1981)

Hood, M. S. F., The Arts of Prehistoric Greece (Harmondsworth, 1978)

Hooker, J. T., *Mycenaean Greece* (New Jersey, 1977)

Hope-Simpson, R. and Dickenson, O. T. P. K., *Gazeteer of Aegean Civilisation in the Bronze Ag*e (Goteborg, 1979)

Mountjoy, P., *Mycenaean Pottery: An Introduction* (Oxford, 1993)

Mylonas, G. E., *Mycenae Rich in Gold* (Athens, 1983)

Preziosi, D. and Hitchcock, L., *Aegean Art and Architecture* (Oxford, 1999)

Taylour, L. W., *The Mycenaeans* (London, 1983)

Vermeule, E., *Greece in the Bronze Age* (Chicago, 1972)

Wardle, K. and Wardle, D., *Cities of Legend: the Mycenaean World* (Bristol, 1997)

Warren, P. M., *The Aegean Civilizations* (Oxford, 1989)

Wood, M., *In Search of the Trojan War* (London, 1985)

EXCELLENT OVERVIEWS WITH DETAILED BIBLIOGRAPHIES AND NOTES

Dickenson, O. T. P. K., *The Aegean Bronze Age* (Cambridge, 1994)

Latacz, J. *Troy and Homer: Towards a Solution of an Old Mystery* (Oxford, 2004)

Shelmerdine, C. W., 'Review of Aegean Prehistory VI: The Palatial Bronze Age of the Southern and Central Greek Mainland', in Cullen, T. (ed.), *Aegean Prehistory: A Review* (Boston, 2001)

A detailed bibliography can be found in the searchable database of *Nestor: Bibliography of Aegean Prehistory and Related Areas* (Department of Classics, University of Cincinnati) http://ucaswww.mcm.ucedu/classics/nestor/nestor.html

SELECTED REGIONAL SURVEYS

Southern Argolid Exploration Project: Jameson, M. H.,

Runnels, C. M. and van Andel, T. H., *A Greek Countryside: The Southern Argolid from Prehistory to the Present Day* (Stanford, 1994)

Nemea Valley Archaeological Project: http://classics.lsa.umich.edu/NVAP.html

Laconia Survey: Cavanagh, W. C. et al., *The Laconia Survey II: Continuity and Change in a Greek Rural Landscape: Archaeological Data* (London, 1996)

EXHIBITION CATALOGUES

Demakopoulou, K. (ed.), *The Mycenaean World: Five Centuries of Early Greek Culture 1600 – 1100 BC* (Athens, 1988)

Tzedakis, I. and Martlew, H., Minoans *and Mycenaeans: Flavours of their Time* (Athens, 1999)

Korfmann, M. (ed.), *Troia. Traum und Wirklichkeit. Wissenschaftlicher Begleitband zur Troia-Ausstellung* (Stuttgart, Braunschweig and Bonn, 2001)

Yalcin, U, Pulak, C. and Slotta, R., *Das Schiff von Uluburun: Welthandel vor 3000 Jahren* (Bochum, 2005)

IMPORTANT COLLECTIONS OF CONFERENCE PAPERS

Bennet, J. and Driessen, J. (eds), *A-na-qo-ta: Studies Presented to J. T. Killen* (Salamanca, 1999)

Branigan, K. (ed.), *Cemetery and Society in the Aegean Bronze Age* (Sheffield, 1998)

Carter, J. B. and Morris, S. P. (eds), *The Ages of Homer* (Austin, 1995)

Davis, J. L. (ed.), *Sandy Pylos: an Archaeological History from Nestor to Navarino* (Austin, 1998)

French, E. and Wardle, K. A. (eds), *Problems in Greek Prehistory* (Bristol, 1986)

Laffineur, R. and Niemeier, W-D. (eds), *Politeia: Society and State in the Aegean Bronze Age* (Liège, 1995)

Laffineur, R. (ed.), *Polemos: Le contexte guerrier en Egée à l'âge du Bronze* (2 vols; Liege, 1999)

Morris, I. and Powell, B. (eds), *A New Companion to Homer* (Leiden, 1997)

Voutsaki, S. and Killen, J. (eds), *Economy and Politics in the Mycenaean Palace States* (Cambridge, 2001)

Acknowledgements

Warmest and heartfelt thanks to Lesley Fitton, without whom this book would probably never have been written, and to Richard Hodges, for being an inspiration.

I would also like to thank Coralie Hepburn and Nina Shandloff at British Museum Press, as well as Carolyn Jones (for comments on the text), Beatriz Walters (for assistance in sourcing illustrations) and Andrew Shoolbred (for design).

Many of my former colleagues in the Department of Greek and Roman Antiquities at the British Museum have been wonderfully helpful, especially Lucilla Burn, Paul Roberts, Kim Overend and Dyfri Williams.

Many thanks to Kate Morton, Candida Lonsdale and Sue Bird for maps and drawings and to Mark Bloomfield, Dominique Collon, Stephen Cooter, Lesley Fitton, George Hart, Brendon O'Connor and John Prag for photographs. The British Museum photographs were taken by 'Nic' Nichols, Ivor Kerslake and Dudley Hubbard.

And finally I would like to thank Brendon O'Connor for his irrepressible enthusiasm and Simon Harrison for his unflagging encouragement and for the happy months I spent in his secret garden writing much of this book.

Illustration acknowledgements

1. Photograph: British Museum, BM Cat. Sculpture 1825

2. From Edward Dodwell, *Classical and Topographical Tour through Greece during the years 1801, 1805, 1806* (London, 1819)

3. From Edward Dodwell, *Views and Descriptions of Cyclopian or Pelasgic Remains in Greece and Italy* (London, 1934)

4. From Heinrich Schliemann, *Ilios: the City and Country of the Trojans* (London, 1880)

5. Photograph: magazine image

6. From Heinrich Schliemann, *Mycenae* (London, 1878)

7. Photograph: British Museum, PD R36365/1

8. Photograph: Louise Schofield

9. Photograph: British Museum, GR 1910. 4-23.1. Drawing: Kate Morton

10. Drawing: Kate Morton

11. Photograph: Louise Schofield

12. Photograph: British Museum, BM Cat. Vases A281, A283 and A284

13. Photograph: Hellenic Republic Ministry of Culture, Archaeological Receipts Fund (T A P Service)

14. Photograph: Hellenic Republic Ministry of Culture, Archaeological Receipts Fund (T A P Service)

15. Photograph: University of Manchester

16. Photograph: University of Manchester

17. Photograph: Hellenic Republic Ministry of Culture, Archaeological Receipts Fund (T A P Service)

18. Photograph: Hellenic Republic Ministry of Culture, Archaeological Receipts Fund (T A P Service)

19. Photograph: C M Dixon/Ancient Art & Architecture Collection Ltd

20. From Heinrich Schliemann, *Mycenae* (London, 1878)

21. Photograph: akg-images/Nimatallah

22. Photograph: akg-images

23. Photograph: akg-images

24. Photograph: Hellenic Republic Ministry of Culture, Archaeological Receipts Fund (T A P Service)

25. Photograph: British Museum, BM Cat. Vases A782, A783 and A754

26. Photograph: J.L. Fitton

27. Photograph: British Museum, BM Cat. Jewellery 820

28. Drawing: Kate Morton

29. Drawing: Kate Morton

30. Photograph: Louise Schofield

31. Photograph: J.L. Fitton

32. Photograph: British Museum, BM Cat. Vases A802 and A803

33. Photograph: Hellenic Republic Ministry of Culture, Archaeological Receipts Fund (T A P Service)

34. Photograph: Louise Schofield

35. Photograph: British Museum, BM Cat. Vases A651 and A981

36. Drawing: Candida Lonsdale

37. Photograph: J.L. Fitton

38. Photograph: George Hart

39. Photograph: British Museum, GR 1959.11-4.1

40. Photograph: Stephen Cooter, BBC

41. Photograph: J.L. Fitton

42. Drawing: Sue Bird, BM Cat. Gems 46

43. Photograph: J.L. Fitton

44. Drawing: Kate Morton

45. Drawing: Kate Morton (after the Mycenae Atlas)

46. Photograph: Louise Schofield

47. Photograph: Louise Schofield

48. Drawing: Candida Lonsdale

49. Drawing: Kate Morton

50. Photograph: Louise Schofield

51. Drawing: Kate Morton

52. Photograph: Hellenic Republic Ministry of Culture, Archaeological Receipts Fund (T A P Service)

53. Drawing: Candida Lonsdale

54. Photograph: Louise Schofield

55. Drawing: Candida Lonsdale

56. Photograph: J.L. Fitton

57. Photograph: British Museum, BM Cat. Bronzes 113

58. Photograph: British Museum, EA 35413 and BM Cat. Vases A987

59. Photograph: British Museum, BM Cat. Vases C341

60. Photograph: British Museum, BM Cat. Vases C416

61. Photograph: R Sheridan/Ancient Art & Architecture Collection Ltd

62. Photograph, British Museum, contents of Tomb 93, Enkomi, Cyprus

63. Photograph: British Museum, GR 1872.3-15. 84, 85 and 88

64. Photograph: Dominique Collon

65. Photograph: British Museum, BM Cat. Vases C342

66. Drawing: Candida Lonsdale

67. Photograph: R Sheridan/Ancient Art & Architecture Collection Ltd

68. Photograph: akg-images

69. Photograph: G T Garvey/ Ancient Art & Architecture Collection Ltd

70. Photograph: British Museum, BM Cat. Bronzes 2 and 2752-4 and GR 1930.12-15.1

71. Photograph: British Museum, BM Cat. Bronzes 19-22 and 29

72. Photograph: British Museum, BM Cat. Bronzes 30 and 31, GR 1872.6-20.15-20, 22 and 23, GR 1872.3-1.61

73. Photograph: British Museum, BM Cat. Vases C333

74. Photograph: British Museum, BM Cat. Terracottas B2 and A22

75. Photograph: British Museum, EA 74100

76. Drawing: Candida Lonsdale

77. Drawing: Candida Lonsdale

78. Photograph: British Museum, BM Cat. Vases C399

79. Drawing: Candida Lonsdale

80. Photograph: British Museum, BM Cat. Jewellery 580

81. Photograph: British Museum, BM Cat. Jewellery 813, BM Cat. Glass 65, GR 1872.3-15.118, 1 and 2, GR 1872.3-15.76,1, GR 1872.3-15.119,2, GR 1872.3-15.6 and 13, BM Cat. Jewellery 811

82. Photograph: British Museum, BM Cat. Glass 28, 31, 35, 44, 49, 55, 66, and 73, GR 1905.6-10.12 and 13, GR 1905.6-10.4 and BM Cat. Gems 63

83. Photograph: British Museum, GR 1872.3-15.82

84. Photograph: British Museum, BM Cat. Jewellery 793 and 794

85. Photograph: British Museum, BM Cat. Jewellery 772

86. Photograph: R Sheridan/Ancient Art & Architecture Collection Ltd

87. Photograph: British Museum, GR 1996.3-25.3

88. Photograph: British Museum, 1996.5-28.1-3, GR 1955.11-23.9

89. Drawing: Candida Lonsdale

90. Photograph: British Museum, BM Cat. Bronzes 38 and 39, GR 1872. 3-15.94, BM Cat. Bronzes 9 and 35, GR 1872.6-20.35

91. Photograph: British Museum, BM Cat. Vases C397

92. Photograph: British Museum, BM Cat. Vases C417

93. Photograph: British Museum, GR 1897.4-1.300

94. Photograph: British Museum, BM Cat. Gems 105 and 61, GR 1934. 11-20.12, BM Cat. Gems 54, GR 1960.10-1.1 and 1966.3-28.26

95. Photograph: British Museum, BM Cat. Vases A 846

96. Photograph: British Museum, BM Cat. Vases A971 and C607

97. Photograph: British Museum, BM Cat. Vases A952, BM Cat. Terracottas B3 and 4

98. Photograph: British Museum, GR 1992.10-15.1 and 1996.3-25.1

99. Photograph: British Museum, BM Cat. Vases A950

100. Photograph: British Museum, BM Cat. Vases C334

101. Photograph: Getty Museum, 85.AE. 145

102. Drawing: Kate Morton

103. Photograph: C M Dixon/Ancient Art & Architecture Collection Ltd

104. Photograph: Hellenic Republic Ministry of Culture, Archaeological Receipts Fund (T A P Service)

105. Photograph: Hellenic Republic Ministry of Culture, Archaeological Receipts Fund (T A P Service)

106. Drawing: Candida Lonsdale

107. Drawing: Candida Lonsdale

108. Photograph: British Museum, GR 1963.7-5.1

109. Photograph: British Museum BM Cat. Sculpture A56; computerized reconstruction: Mark Bloomfield

110. Computerized reconstruction: Mark Bloomfield

111. Photograph: British Museum, BM Cat. Bronzes 15

112. BM Cat. Terracottas B11, B12 and B5

113. Photograph: British Museum, BM Cat. Vases A1008, C608 and A870

114. Drawing: Candida Lonsdale

115. Photograph: Hellenic Republic Ministry of Culture, Archaeological Receipts Fund (T A P Service)

116. Photograph: Louise Schofield

117. Photograph: Stephen Cooter, BBC

118. Photograph: George Hart

119. Photograph: British Museum, GR 1897.4-1.883

120. Drawing: Sue Bird

121. Photograph: Brendon O'Connor

Index

Numbers in *italics* refer to illustrations